A Fresh Look at Confession

A *Fresh Look* at
Confession

...why it **really is** good for the soul

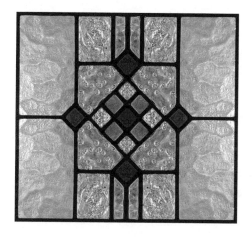

DAVID M. KNIGHT

TWENTY
THIRD *23rd*
PUBLICATIONS
NEW LONDON, CT 06320
WWW.23RDPUBLICATIONS.COM

TWENTY-THIRD PUBLICATIONS

A Division of Bayard

One Montauk Avenue, Suite 200

New London, CT 06320

(860) 437-3012 or (800) 321-0411

www.23rdpublications.com

ISBN: 978-1-58595-901-3

Library of Congress Control Number: 2012953612

Printed in the U.S.A.

TABLE OF CONTENTS

Introduction

CONFESSION IS A MYSTICAL EXPERIENCE

I was forty years a priest before I realized that priests don't hear sins in Confession.

We hear *ideals*. In fact, we are listening to people's mystical experiences, even though they may be conscious only of confessing their sins.

Here's an example. Suppose you accuse yourself of using bad language. There is no great revelation in that. Everybody you live or work with knows you cuss, takes it for granted, and assumes you do too. But if you mention it in Confession, the priest learns something nobody else knows: you are someone who actually disapproves of cussing; it is contrary to your personal ideals. In your heart you have a higher ideal than appears in your behavior. This is a revelation of grace — and of identity.

You need to know this. You probably feel bad about yourself because of your foul mouth. But the truth is, you can't look down on anything unless something in you has risen

above it. So what you really discover by confessing your sin
— but possibly won't unless the confessor points it out to
you — is that your heart is on a higher moral level than your
mouth. And so are you as a person. Strange as it sounds, one
of the principal reasons for confessing our sins is to realize
how good we are!

To realize we have the same ideals as God is a mystical
experience. If that phrase frightens you, call it an *experience
of grace*. They are one and the same thing. When you become
aware that you personally are judging an action the way God
does — you are not just parroting what you were taught as a
child, but see for yourself that it is wrong because God within you is showing you that it is — you are experiencing both
the action of God in your heart and your response to God's
action, God's gift of light and your acceptance of God's gift.
That is a mystical experience.

FROM RELIGION TO SPIRITUALITY

Seeing Confession this way takes it out of the box of *religion*
— defined as conformity to a system of doctrines, rules, and
practices — and puts it into the area of *spirituality* — experienced interaction with God.

We enter into a conscious spiritual life on the day we realize that *something is going on* between ourselves and God,
and decide to get involved in it.

Our religion becomes our spirituality when we embrace
its doctrines as truth revealed to us by a God we personally
choose to believe in, follow its rules as guidance from a God
whose way we have explicitly decided to trust, and engage

in its practices as an interchange of love with a God we consciously desire to be close to.

If our experience of Confession is not all of the above, we have not yet assimilated its meaning or fully experienced its mystery. The goal of this book is to help you use and experience Confession as an encounter that draws you closer to God.

CHAPTER ONE

The Sacrament
of Self-Identity

Experiencing oneself as a Christian

CONFESSION OF SIN – PROFESSION OF FAITH

T he truth is that every confession of sin is more profoundly a profession of faith.

What Christians began to call the "sacrament" ("mystery") of Reconciliation began in a very human way. Sometimes, when they were threatened with torture and death in times of persecution, Christians denied their faith. When they showed up to celebrate Eucharist again with the community after being released from prison, the other Christians did not know what to make of them.

"What are you doing here? You don't believe in Jesus."

"Of course I believe in Jesus. I am a Christian."

"But you denied him. You told the Romans you did not believe in him."

One answer to this might be, "Did you see the teeth on those lions?"

If this is the reply given by the *apostate* (from *stasis*: "standing" and *apo*: "away" — one who "stands away" from the community, takes a stance "apart from" the Church), it might well mean that, in fact, the person not only denied the faith but never had it in the first place. Anyone who does not believe we should bear witness to Jesus through the sacrifice of our life — and of every other good on earth — does not really believe in him as God, and does not accept the "first and greatest commandment": "You shall love the Lord your God with *all* your heart, and with *all* your soul..." (Matthew 22:37). Such a person might fit into the group John describes:

> They went out from us, but they did not belong to us; for if they had belonged to us, they would have remained with us. But by going out they made it plain that none of them belonged to us. (1 John 2:19)

However, such an answer might also mean, "Hey, I was just scared. I know I should have given up my life in witness to Jesus (the actual meaning of *martyr* in Greek is *witness*), but I was terrified. I was wrong. I was a coward. I sinned."

In this case, the *confession of sin* would be a *profession of faith*. If the community judged it to be sincere, the apostate could be reconciled with them and accepted back into the fellowship of the believers as a participant in Eucharist.

This judgment did not happen through majority vote. It was made by the one who, as head of the community or local "church" (the word *church* means *assembly)*, could speak in the name of all. That was the bishop.[1]

For the sake of morale, however, reconciliation was not granted until the returning apostates had given visible proof that this time their profession of faith was real. Their faith had not been strong enough to hold up against torture before; could they be believed now?

In the early Church proof of faith took the form of a long and rigorous public penance imposed by the bishop — like standing outside the door of the church in sackcloth and ashes for years, or being required to live only on alms. The penance had to be completed before the bishop would grant absolution and readmit the penitent to full participation in Eucharist. If, however, during one of the times of recurring, intermittent persecution, someone who was actually imprisoned and facing death for the faith — already called a martyr — would intercede for the penitent, the penance might be mitigated or shortened. This was called an *indulgence.* An indulgence was nothing but the bishop's choice to grant relief from a penalty he himself had imposed.

And so the practice of what we now call *sacramental confession* was born.

On the one hand, it was a very human process — even a juridical one. Someone with *jurisdiction,* or the right to speak in the name of the community, judged whether the apostate's confession of sin was a sincere profession of regret based on faith, and whether the sinner, in spite of weakness, was really committed to the truth and values of Christ. Public penance was required as proof. When credibility was reestablished, the local head of the assembly, the bishop, declared the sinner freed or absolved from any obstacle to full participation in the life of the community of faith. All the other members were committed to accept his judgment. The breach was healed, unity was restored, and the morale of the community — weakened by doubts about how much trust they could place in the sincerity of the communal profession of faith that bound them together — was strengthened.

FOR THE SAKE OF COMMUNITY

We notice that the common good of the community, and not the individual's relationship to God, was the original goal of Confession in the reconciliation process. While an individual's personal and private relationship to God was certainly an issue, the main focus remained the benefit of a community's restored assurance about their common unity in faith and values. The only sins confessed were public ones that were experienced as a disruption of the *koinonia*, the experienced fellowship or "communion in the Holy Spirit" that was so important for "building up the Church" (1 Corinthians 14:12–26). At first just apostasy was confessed. Later, known murder and adultery were included.

Does this mean that the reconciliation of penitents was nothing but a matter of healing wounds in the community's morale? Was it simply a human and juridical process that served an organizational purpose?

To answer that question — and to understand Confession today — we have to go deeper into the mystery of our redemption.

A TRIPLE MYSTERY

When the *lapsi* (those who had "lapsed" in their profession of the faith) were reconciled with the community, a mystery was being enacted on a level deeper than outward appearance. The visible reintegration of the apostate into the community expressed an invisible reintegration into the divine life of the Body of Christ. The mystery of redemption and the mystery of sacramental reconciliation are one and the same. They are the same mystery as Baptism.

We were "saved" at Baptism by being incorporated, with all of our sins — past, present, and future — into the body of Jesus hanging on the cross. Since Jesus died almost two thousand years before we existed, this may be a confusing point. It might help if we think in terms of the difference between how we and God perceive time.

We live in *linear* time. For us, the past is over, the future does not yet exist, and only the present is real. But for God, all of time is present in one eternal "now." Using imagery, we could say that God sees time as a circle, the way we see the moon. Every event on the circumference of the circle, from the beginning of time to the end, is present to him in one view. And at the center of the circle is the cross.

Christ's death and rising are the timeless moment without which no moment of time has meaning, for "in him all things in heaven and on earth were created...all things have been created through him and for him. He himself is before all things, and in him all things hold together" (Colossians 1:16–17). Nothing was created except in view of the final reintegration of all things in Christ.

For this reason, the sacrifice of Jesus on Calvary, though it took place in time, is a timeless moment. As Priest and Victim Jesus transcends time.

> He holds his priesthood permanently, because he continues forever. Consequently he is able *for all time* to save those

who approach God through him, since *he always lives to make intercession for them.*" (Hebrews 7:24–25)

It clarifies things to picture Jesus hanging on the cross at the center of the circle of time. Jesus died in time and space, at a point along the circumference of the circle, on the hill of Calvary outside Jerusalem, around the year 33 AD. But in reality (God's reality), his death was and is at the center of time. All human history revolves around that moment. It was in view of our redemption on Calvary that the human race was created. And every human life, no matter when it begins or ends, wherever it is positioned along the circumference of the circle, whether before or after the period of Jesus' life on earth, has the death and resurrection of Jesus as its center.

We are all equidistant from the cross.

When we were baptized, we were baptized "into" that body hanging on the cross at the center of time. We, with all of our sins, were incorporated into his body. As we became members of Jesus' own body, our sins became the sins of Jesus' own flesh. He "became sin" for us. "For our sakes God made him who did not know sin to be sin, so that in him we might become the very holiness of God" (2 Corinthians 5:21).

When Jesus died, we died in him. We, with all of our sins, went down into the grave with him, and our sins were annihilated. Then we rose in him and returned to earth to take our place again on the circumference of the circle as a "new creation."

All of us who have been baptized into Christ Jesus were baptized into his death. Therefore we have been buried with him by baptism into death, so that, just as Christ was raised from the dead by the glory of the Father, so we too might walk in newness of life. (Romans 6:3–4)

"LAMB OF GOD"

The mystery of redemption is that, in Jesus, the "Lamb of God," our sins are not just forgiven but *"taken away."*

> The next day John saw Jesus coming toward him and declared, "Here is the Lamb of God who *takes away* the sin of the world!" (John 1:29)

Because we died in Christ, no reality or record of our guilt remains. The one who committed those sins died. "If anyone is in Christ, there is a *new creation*: everything old has passed away; see, everything has become new!" (2 Corinthians 5:17).

> When you were buried with him in baptism, you were also raised with him through faith in the power of God, who raised him from the dead....God made you alive together with him, when he forgave us all our trespasses, *erasing the record* that stood against us....He set this aside, nailing it to the cross. (Colossians 2:12–14)

What happened on Calvary, what happened at our Baptism, and what happens in the sacrament of Reconciliation are all the same mystery: the mystery of being taken, incorporated, or reintegrated into the body of Jesus on the cross, dying with and in him, and rising with and in him as free of all guilt as if we had never sinned in our lives.

Catholics celebrate the Immaculate Conception of Mary as the belief that the flesh of Jesus, the Incarnate Word of God, could never have been under the power of sin at any moment of its existence. This leads to the conclusion that the flesh of Mary, in order to become the flesh of God, must have been preserved from all corruption by sin from the first moment of her conception in her mother's womb.

But if Jesus, after being born, was "made sin" by incorporating us, with all of our sins, into his body, it stands to reason that this could only be in view of overcoming sin completely by taking the "sins of the world" into his flesh in order to annihilate them.

The Church sees Mary as the "preview and promise" of the Church in its perfection. What Mary was, all of us will be when the process of redemption is complete. The perfection we see in her is a preview of our own. So Father Karl Rahner, SJ, wrote that Mary's Immaculate Conception is a sign and promise that we will all be "immaculately conceived" when our rebirth through the death and rising of our Baptism is brought to perfection at the end of our lives. Before we enter heaven, we all will be as totally and perfectly purified of all sin as if we had never, ever, sinned in our life.

> Christ loved the Church and gave himself up for her, in order to *make her holy* by cleansing her with the washing of water by the word, so as to present the Church to himself in splendor, *without a spot or wrinkle or anything of the kind* — yes, so that she may be *holy and without blemish.* (Ephesians 5:25–27; Colossians 1:21–22)

In our linear, earthly time frame we see Baptism as taking away all of our sins up to that moment. But in God's time frame our future sins were also annihilated in Christ's death. So in the sacrament of Reconciliation — which takes place in our linear time — we confess, we give to Christ, we include, all the sins we have committed since Baptism (or since our last Confession). But God already sees us as we will see ourselves and one another at the "end time" when Jesus presents us to himself "in splendor, without a spot or wrinkle or anything of the kind...holy and without blemish." Being purified of sin in Reconciliation brings our time frame into harmony with God's.

The "sacramental" encounter

Visibly, the bishop's absolution reintegrated apostates into the human community of believers on earth. Invisibly, they were restored to live in union with Christ the Head by renewed sharing in the divine life of his mystical body on earth.

That is why Baptism and Reconciliation are called sacraments. A sacrament is an invisible interaction with God embodied in a visible interaction with human beings. God can give grace through direct, spiritual interaction with anyone, without using any created intermediaries, means, words, or gestures at all. But in Jesus, God healed, enlightened, and saved people, not only through human words and touches, but by using bread, wine, water, blood, even mud and saliva! (see John 9:6). What we call a "sacramental grace" is a grace (a life-giving "favor" from God) that comes to us through particular physical signs and visible interaction with human beings. So, in sacramental Reconciliation, union with God is restored through the visible sign of restored union with the human community of believers.

Three practical conclusions

We have gone into deep theology here, which means deep mystery. On the practical level, there are three important things we should be sure we have absorbed:

❶ Our sins no longer exist

In Baptism and Confession, our sins are not just "forgiven" but *taken away*. The difference is crucial. With no pun intended, the "crux" of our redemption is the cross.

Forgiveness doesn't change us. The one who forgives becomes more loving, more godlike by that act. But the one forgiven is just as guilty as before.

If Jesus only "paid the price of our sins," our sins would still be part of us. God would just be "overlooking" them. But the truth is, we are not delivered from sin by Jesus dying *for us*, but by the mystery of *our* dying *in him*. We may not have been clear about this mystery.

That is why people do not always find peace in Confession. It may be a relief to know God doesn't hold something against us and (if such is our understanding of God) that we will not be "punished" for what we have done. But forgiveness doesn't change the fact that we did what we did. And if it is something that makes it hard for us to live with ourselves, we continue to carry the crushing weight of our sin.

I learned this the hard way. When I was a missionary in Africa, I killed a sixteen-year-old girl in an automobile accident. It was my fault. Obviously, I didn't mean to kill her, so what I was technically guilty of was a "venial sin" of impatience that made me careless. However, the difference between "venial" and "mortal" sin doesn't mean much when someone is lying dead in the road.

I duly confessed my sin and its consequence, and didn't feel any better at all. I knew God had forgiven me, but I was still the man who killed that girl, and all the forgiveness in the world could not take that away.

For mental health reasons, I chose to put this out of my

mind for two years. Then I made a thirty-day retreat and confronted it. The first words that came to my mind were "Christ became a curse for us, hanging on the tree." This was followed by the verse: "For our sakes God made him who did not know sin to *be sin*, so that in him we might become the very holiness of God" (see Galatians 3:13; 2 Corinthians 5:21).

Jesus took me, with all of my sins, into his body on the cross. When he died, I died in him. I thought of Paul's words: "Do you not know that all of us who have been baptized into Christ Jesus were baptized into his death?"

I went down into the grave with Christ, as I went down into the waters of Baptism. My sins were buried with me. When Jesus rose, I rose in him, leaving my sins behind:

> Therefore we have been buried with him by baptism into death, so that, just as Christ was raised from the dead by the glory of the Father, so we too might walk in newness of life.
>
> So if anyone is in Christ, there is a *new creation*: everything old has passed away; see, everything has become new! (Romans 6:3–4; 2 Corinthians 5:17)

That is the mystery of redemption — Jesus does not just forgive; he "takes away" the sins of the world. And he does it as the Lamb of God, by dying and incorporating us into his death. Because we have died in Christ, there is no record of our sin, either in heaven or (in God's eyes) on earth! The one who committed those sins *died*. We live now as the risen body of Jesus. We are a new creation. If we continue to hold on to the memory of our sins, what we are holding onto is something we have robbed from Jesus Christ. On the cross he said, "Give me your sins by giving me yourself." He died so that we might die in him and our sins be annihilated. It is wrong to rob him of the fruit of his passion and death by taking back the burden he died to take away.

❷ Sin and reconciliation are communal

There is always a communal dimension, both to sin and to reconciliation. We cannot sin against God without sinning against other human beings. And we cannot seek reconciliation with God without involving other human beings. "So when you are offering your gift at the altar," Jesus says, "if you remember that your brother or sister has something against you, leave your gift there before the altar and go; first be reconciled to your brother or sister, and then come and offer your gift" (Matthew 5:23–24). We might not like the idea of confessing our sins to the Church. But if we do not — in some form or another — we are leaving things unfinished when we confess them to God.

When we acknowledge our sins to the Church, we are reaffirming — and in that act reexperiencing, deepening, and reinforcing — our identity as co-responsible *members* of the community of faith. We are in the Church. We truly belong, and accept our belonging, as members committed to give as well as to receive. In the maturity of our relationship with other believers we recognize that we owe it to the community, as well as to God, to live in a way that makes our profession of faith credible. When we fail to do this — as all of us do to some extent — we recognize the need to *repair*. We undo the damage our sins have caused either to the community's morale or simply to our own ability to contribute to the community's mission. We do this through a confession of sins that is a public profession of faith. Although the actual confession is in private, the fact that we "turn ourselves in," as my irreverent cousin used to say, by going into the confessional, is a public act. And in the sacrament we confess to the priest as a representative of the community. In that act we experience our identity as believing, committed members of the fellowship (*koinonia*) of the body of Christ.

❸   Confession is an expression and experience of faith

The real focus of Confession is not on our "works" but on our *faith*. We only confess the failure of our works in order to reaffirm — and in the process experience — the presence within us of a live faith by which we judge them. In Confession we recognize the light in our hearts when we see it revealing to us the darkness of our behavior. Therefore, we should prepare for Confession by looking at our lives in the light of the word of God and of his Spirit abiding in our hearts. What we are getting in touch with is less the reality of our sins (no great mystery there!) and more the reality of God's enlightening, inviting, inspiring action in our hearts. Confession should be a mystical experience.

Like the disciples who met Jesus on the road after his resurrection but only recognized him "in the breaking of the bread," we look back after the "breaking open" of our hearts and say, "Were not our hearts burning within us while he was talking to us on the road...?" (Luke 24:32).

We look back on our lives and realize, "The only reason I knew or felt that what I was doing was sin was because God was enlightening me. I have been in live contact with God. I just didn't recognize it at the time." That is mystical experience. It is the experience of knowing something, not because you see it with your eyes or understand it with your intellect, but because it is more real to you than that.

It may be something you were taught, something you have thought about and understand, something that "makes sense" to you. But when you get in touch with yourself, you realize you do not accept it just because it makes sense to you. Your acceptance is deeper than that. You know it on a level deeper than mere intellectual understanding. You know that this truth, this ideal, is part of you. Knowing it, believing it, and accepting it are part of what you are.

And it is part of you by grace: because of your participation in the divine life of God.

This is an experience of grace. Whether you consciously think of it that way or not, it is an experience of *sharing in the divine life of God*. By the gift of faith you are sharing in God's own act of knowing. By the gift of hope you are setting your heart on what God holds out to you and believing it is possible; you are sharing in God's own awareness, sharing firsthand in God's own intention to keep his promises. And by the gift of love you love what God loves, desire what God desires, appreciate what God appreciates.

When you examine your conscience in preparation for Confession, you are really examining your *consciousness*. You are recognizing and acknowledging as your own what God is sharing with you of his own truth, his own values, his own ideals. You are discovering your true self, your deep identity, as a graced person, someone who shares in the divine light and life of God.

Your confession of sin is the act in which this is *realized* (becomes real) and is recognized by being embodied in action. What you are really revealing is your ideals. This is all about who you really are, not what you have done. The real you has a different set of ideals, reflecting your heart instead of your lapses. This you abides with God.

Confessions are mystical experiences for the priest or confessor as well. Confessors get to hear how good people are when they think they are revealing how bad they are! To hear confessions is to perceive the action of God in the human race — God speaking to people, raising them to his level of ideals, and their responding to him. It is a very encouraging experience. It should be even more encouraging for those who realize, in the confession of their sins, how real is their profession of faith.

CHAPTER TWO

The Sacrament *of the* Examined Life

Experiencing oneself as a disciple

Socrates said, "The unexamined life is not worth living." We can experience ourselves as living life like a pinball. We are shot out of the womb into a maze of interaction with things and people. We have no built-in course. Unless we set one, we can spend our lives bouncing blindly off of one encounter after another, lighting up unplanned points on the screen, until we finally drop meaninglessly into the grave.

Or we can set a course. Unlike the pinball, we have a capacity for self-direction. If we have been given the gift of faith we can choose a *way* based on *truth* that leads to *life* in its fullness. That is the "life to the full" promised by Jesus, who identified himself as "the Way, and the Truth, and the Life" (John 10:10; 14:6).

To choose this intentional course is to take on the identity of a *disciple*.

"Disciple" does not mean "follower." It means *student*. We can think we are following Jesus all our lives by blindly following the "Christian crowd," living by the rules and practices of our particular religious culture in an unexamined way, just doing what we have been taught to do. Socrates would call this a life not worth living.

Or we can choose to be students of the mind and heart of Christ — Christians who intentionally follow his way, interiorly enlightened by his truth, consciously experiencing his life. This is to live the "examined life" of disciples.

In Confession we have a sacrament of the examined life.

Confession is something built into our lifestyle that calls us to examine our lives periodically, because it is a standing invitation to give an account of them. Someone is provided by our church or otherwise made available who is ready and willing to listen: a *confessor*. This might be an ordained minister or simply a wise, experienced friend. Our confession might be sacramental or not. But its special healing and life-enhancing power requires that it be confession to another human being. (The fifth step of Alcoholics Anonymous is proof of this principle.) Whatever form it takes, it is functionally a support for the examined life.

Earlier, we saw that Confession began as an expression of *return*. Those who were distanced from the Christian community by behavior incompatible with its faith reaffirmed their faith through acknowledgment of their sin as sin and were reintegrated into the community. Today, for those who make Confession a regular part of their life, it is most often an expression of *concern*. It is a way of realizing — in both senses: of discovering and making real — that one is seriously concerned about living the Christian life in a full and authentic way. What people confess are not acts of abandoning the way of Christ, but momentary (or even habitual) lapses in following it. They confess wobbles in their course, weakness in their performance, "falls" like "falling down on the job" — a break in forward motion.

People are sometimes shocked when I say that in more than forty-eight years of hearing confessions — on six continents — I have very rarely heard anything I judged to be a true mortal sin. (I will explain later that the real mortal sins are seldom confessed — those sins that destroy lives and devastate the quality of human life on earth are the last to be faced and acknowledged.)

What priests hear in ordinary confessions are the ordinary sins that do damage, sometimes serious damage, to the way people live individually and together. But the damage is rarely so great — or subjectively appreciated as being so great — that the people who commit those sins are killing the divine life of God within themselves. Their sins are not "deadly." To commit what John calls "mortal sin" (1 John 5:16–17), we have to do something that is not just bad, even seriously bad, but *evil*. We have to embrace a course of action so evil in itself that it is totally incompatible with sharing in the divine life of God. John says this is always a withholding of the fundamental gift of love. "Whoever does not love," he wrote, "abides in death" (1 John 3:14).

THE "EXAMINATION OF CONSCIENCE"

We can prepare for Confession on different levels. The way that used to be most common was to go through a "laundry list" supplied in catechisms and prayer books, looking for anything we had done that the "canned conscience" listed as sins. These were usually concrete actions, simplistically cut-and-dried, and predictably superficial: "Did I tell any lies, steal anything, use bad language?" "Lying" did not go into the destructive deceptiveness of "spin," of advertisements reinforcing false values, or the subtle manipulation of family or friends. "Stealing" did not include the luxury spending that the reflective Church calls "stealing from the poor," or exploitative and irresponsible business practices that strip thousands of their jobs and savings. "Bad language" did not make anyone think of the irresponsible use of words that perpetuate harmful stereotypes, such as "sexist" language. It did not include using nicknames that lower another's self-image, or pretentious titles that falsely enhance it. (No one has ever confessed it as "bad language" to address a bishop as "Your Excellency"!)

Since the Second Vatican Council (1962–1965), those who make regular use of Confession have begun to go beyond the "checklist" examination of sins. They are much more likely to talk about what kind of *person* they see themselves becoming, using concrete failures as examples. And they tend to accuse themselves in more general but more inclusive ways of neglecting values not specifically in focus in the old days, such as involvement in social action, responsibility toward the poor, egotism and failures in personal relationship with Jesus and others.

A priest whose experience of hearing confessions spans the "then" and the "now" put it this way:

> One might have thought that the way penitents share their sins could not change. Sin is sin, after all. But when I hear a person begin by saying something like, "I've been working on my tendency to take issues from work out on my wife," I

then know we are not in the pre-Vatican II Church anymore. "I'm working on..."—a phrase I never heard in that earlier, supposedly Eden-like era. This is the language of a person who is no longer thinking and speaking in catalogue fashion (two from column one, one from column two) but clearly is engaged in an ongoing process of spiritual search. "I've been trying to vary my way of praying." Or "I'm wrestling with my need to be more trusting of the Lord, who has been faithful to his word again and again in my life." [When I hear this] I think, "*I need to remove my sandals, this is sacred ground!*" (George Wilson, SJ, *America,* May 21, 2007)

What is happening is that Confession is revealing the fruits of an examined life. Personal reflection, guided by Scripture reading and discussion, is opening new doors to wider horizons, more challenging ideals, deeper self-knowledge, and higher levels of faith experience. To those who are *disciples*, students of his mind and heart as revealed in his word, Jesus said, "You will know the truth. And the truth will make you free" — free from the minimal narrowness of codified laws, free from the distorted assumptions of cultural conditioning, free from the inadequacy of others' predigested insights, no matter how brilliant and penetrating they are. By sitting at the feet of the Master himself, we will learn directly from his mouth the Truth we ourselves need to absorb in order to find the Way we ourselves must follow if we want to live "life to the full" in our own particular time, space and circumstances (John 8:32; 10:10; 14:6).

Doing this gives us the mystical experience of *enlightenment*. We experience the prayer that St. Paul made for his disciples being answered in us: "I pray that you may have the power to comprehend, with all the saints, what is the *breadth and length and height and depth*, and to know the love of Christ that surpasses knowledge, so that you may be filled with all the fullness of God" (Ephesians 3:18–19).

Confession is being recognized and used today as the specific tool of *disciples*: those whose life is characterized by reflection on the mind and heart of God. When disciples prepare for Confession (bearing in mind that the preparation itself is an act of discipleship), they examine their lives in the light of what they have read and reflected on in Scripture. They confess their responses to what they have discerned in their hearts as the voice of God.

This makes Confession, and the preparation for it, an experience of graced enlightenment, of experiencing guidance from the word of God and the Holy Spirit instead of just from laws or the example of others.

But it took a few centuries for Confession to evolve to this level.

THE RISE AND FALL OF "PRIVATE CONFESSION"

Historically, the slow transformation of Confession from being an expression of return to being primarily an expression of concern surfaced in Spain around the sixth century, spread to Ireland, and then through Europe. Very gradually an awareness had been growing among Christians that "apartness" from the Church could be caused and expressed by more acts than the three that were originally confessed: apostasy, murder, and adultery. People began to realize that all sins are, to some degree, "apostasy" in the sense of *apo stasis*, standing outside of, apart from the community. Some became seriously worried about whether they had, in fact, lost the life of grace by sins that were not public knowledge. For reassurance they began to bare their souls to the hermit monks who in Ireland dotted the countryside. These were for the most part not ordained, but it was from penitents' adoption of these monks as "spiritual fathers" that the title "father" eventually came to be given to ordained priests.

When Seamus O'Malley stole the widow Murphy's only cow, it began to worry him. "This," he thought, "does not seem consistent with being a Christian. Perhaps I do not really have the faith or the love — especially the love — that belong to the life of grace. How do I know I have not lost the divine life of God? Maybe I am going to Hell!"

When Seamus, for peace of soul, sought out a monk and confided to him that he had stolen the widow Murphy's cow, the monk agreed that, yes, he had a problem. Stealing a poor widow's only cow is inconsistent with Christian love. The monk then began to examine with Seamus why he did it. What was lacking in his understanding of the Gospel? How much deadly attachment did he have to wealth or to the things of this world? What could he do to make the true goal of his life the one he had accepted at Baptism? What means would he have to use to arrive at this — besides giving back the cow?

When Seamus put himself under the monk's guidance, the monk led him through a process that we might call today an unofficial discipline of penance. Seamus did penance in the real sense of engaging in various practices and types of prayer that would help him arrive at *metanoia*, which we translate inadequately as "repentance," but which really means a "complete makeover" of attitudes, values, and behavior.

The process might require a longer or shorter time. But when both Seamus and the monk were satisfied that he was sufficiently converted, they would in some way celebrate together his liberation from sin. This did not necessarily entail sacramental absolution, but it gave Seamus the peace of soul he was looking for.

Notice the change in the purpose of Confession. It was no longer a public re-acceptance given by the bishop to someone known to have "stood apart" from the Church through public apostasy, murder, or adultery. Its purpose was more personal than communal. It was deliverance from an interior, secret weight of guilt for the sake of individual peace of soul. And the process was private rather than public.

The penance the monks required of their penitents was no longer designed to be a *public proof* of conversion to bolster community morale. Now the penance was designed to bring about deep, personal *conversion of heart.* For the penitents this was an acceptance and experience of *discipleship* under the guidance of a spiritual father.

Eventually the bishops merged the old and the new practices of confessing sin. They delegated to ordained priests the right to speak officially in the name of the bishop, allowing them to grant absolution from sins that called one's membership in the community and participation in Eucharist into question. At the same time, they allowed the whole reconciliation process to take place through secret confession, with private penances imposed by the confessor instead of the rigorous public penances the Church used to require before accepting scandalous sinners back into good standing. This had both advantages and disadvantages.

One result of the change was, eventually, a distortion of the sacrament.

THE SLIDE INTO "MAKING SATISFACTION"

❶   Because the process was private, the benefit of restoring *koinonia* was diminished or obscured, especially because the penance was no longer designed to be a public proof of conversion.

❷   Many of the ordinary priests empowered to hear confessions and grant absolution were not educated or spiritual enough to make the penance they imposed a real, effective means of bringing about deeper conversion of heart. So they asked for help that would dispense them from providing the personal guidance they were not equipped to give. In response, some well-meaning fools wrote collections of "canned penances" actually called "*penitentiaries*," that assigned to each category of sin the "punishment that fit the crime."

❸   In time, in the absence of any relationship between the penance and effective conversion of heart, the sacramental penance appeared to be just punishment or satisfaction made to God for sins. Now God was perceived as a punisher. This opened the door to the projection of Purgatory as a place where you "paid for" sins already forgiven (which is not the true doctrine of the Church). This led to a focus on *indulgences*, which now came to be understood, not as the Church's mitigation of penances she herself had imposed, but as dispensations the Church was empowered to grant from all or part of the punishment God was presumed to be exacting in some intermediary holding area between earth and heaven called Purgatory. From there everything went downhill, ending in the perceived "selling" of indulgences that fueled the Protestant Reformation.

The penances ordinarily assigned in Confession today are nothing but a token gesture. They have neither the value of making one's conversion credible to the community nor the value of bringing about true conversion of heart. They are perceived simply as partial payment of a supposed debt of punishment due for sins already forgiven. This is a distortion of Catholic doctrine as well as of the true personality of God. In any treatment of Confession, the less said about "punishment," "satisfaction," "indulgences," or "Purgatory," the better.[1]

THE SACRAMENT OF DISCIPLESHIP

Confession is not just "the sacrament of the examined life"; it is the sacrament of the examined *Christian* life. It is the sacrament of recognized *enlightenment.* The life we embraced and committed ourselves to live at Baptism was the life of *disciples* — students and imitators of the life of Jesus Christ.

Disciples are students of the Word by the Gift of the Holy Spirit. Disciples are more than imitators: our commitment as Christians is to let Jesus himself live and continue his mission in us as in his own body on earth. There is no way to do this unless we commit ourselves to deep, constant, and lifelong *reflection* on the mind and heart of God as revealed in the words and actions of Jesus. We simply *must* be disciples.

This means we must go beyond the rules and practices of our "religion" — those obligatory or customary observances that Paul would lump together as the "Law."

Laws are both the end result and the end of a thinking process. They end it! Congress debates about laws until the vote is cast. Then everyone stops thinking and just starts doing what has been legislated. If we reduce our religion to keeping its laws, we may never think again. But discipleship is a commitment to think.

This means going beyond laws by getting in touch with the source of every Christian law, which is the mind and heart of Christ. It is possible to do this without reading Scripture — for almost fifteen hundred years before the printing press was invented, the mass of Christian believers could not read — but today, when almost everyone can read and copies of the Bible are available to all, we have to ask a question we didn't think to ask before: For those who can read, is reading the Bible a moral *obligation*? Can anyone who chooses not to read the word of God on a regular basis consistently claim to be living an authentic Christian life and to be a disciple of Jesus Christ?

Many Catholics got into the habit of going to Mass on Sunday just because it was a law. We hope they continue for better reasons than that. But does the Church have to make a *law* to convince us we should read the *word of God*? Would anyone seriously argue against the proposition that we have just as much obligation to make Scripture reading a significant part of our lives as we do to go to church on Sunday?

Nevertheless, it is rare to hear people accuse themselves in Confession of not reading the Bible.

A more authentic understanding of Confession will of necessity lead us to prepare for it, to "examine our consciences," by reflecting on Scripture. We will judge our conduct, not by the minimal standards codified in laws, but by the New Law of Christ as proclaimed in the Gospels and probed by Paul. Our basic guide for the "examined life" to which Confession invites us will be the Sermon on the Mount.

As Christians form the habit of going to the words of God

himself for guidance, they will convert from living by laws to living by the Spirit. They will experience their Christian life as a growing *enlightenment* that reaches conscious recognition in the self-discovery of Confession. This is the mystical experience of being the light of the world (Matthew 5:14). This is how Christians will also grow from *studying* as *disciples* into bearing *witness* as *prophets*.

In the next chapter we look at how that changes our experience of Confession.

Chapter Three

The Sacrament *of the* Spirit

Experiencing oneself as a prophet

T he "tokenization" of the penance assigned in Confession invites us to speculate about how its true value could be restored.

The two historical goals of sacramental penance in Christian spirituality were: 1. to give *public proof* of sincere commitment in faith; 2. to achieve personal *conversion of heart*. These can and must be combined.

John Paul II reminded us that sacramental penances are not "a price one pays for sin absolved and forgiveness obtained.... That is the fruit of Christ's precious blood....They are the *sign of the personal commitment* that the Christian has made to God in the sacrament to *begin a new life*. And therefore they should not be reduced to mere formulas to be recited..."[1]

To make one's lifestyle a *visible sign* of personal and empowered commitment to the new life of Christ present in the world is what it means to be a *prophet*.

A "NEW EVANGELIZATION"

We might think of our age in the Church as an "age of witness." We could toy with historical schematization by suggesting that the Church began with a focus on *evangelization*, passed into absorption in *discipleship* as the great theological systems were formed and classic spiritual writings publicized, and now is feeling most urgently called to bear Christian *witness* in order to restore credibility to both of the above. As a historical analysis this is probably of little worth, but it does have some value as a practical point of view.

We are in a time of widespread disbelief that is evoking a Christian counter-renewal. Atheism and agnosticism are taken for granted in some countries and in some cultural strata in ours. Many younger people are turning away from "religion" as they perceive it or have experienced it in Christianity, and are looking elsewhere for "spirituality." The more theological, "liturgical churches" are losing numbers to certain "whoop-it-up," shallow evangelicals. Many who profess to be Christians are unchurched.

The bishops in the Second Vatican Council acknowledged that "more than a little" blame for "the rise of atheism" can be laid at the door of believers: "To the extent that we are careless about our instruction in the faith, or present its teaching falsely, or even fail in our religious, moral, or social life, we must be said to conceal rather than to reveal the true nature of God and of religion."[2]

This statement has personal poignancy for me, as my eldest brother fled in terror more than sixty years ago from the "monster God" who lurked behind the moral teachings we received. Told that God would send a small child to Hell for all eternity for missing Mass on a single Sunday, my brother drew the obvious conclusion: God is unbelievably cruel — and therefore unbelievable. He has been an agnostic ever since.

It is my hope — and my belief — that when my brother dies, his "judgment" will consist in this dialogue:

God: "You didn't believe in me."

My brother: "No, I didn't."

God: "Well, if you had believed that I really was the kind of God you thought I was, that would have been blasphemy. So I am letting you into heaven for not believing that I could be that kind of God."

According to the Council bishops, my brother is only one of many that we have driven out of the Church by "presenting its teaching falsely" in a way that "conceals rather than reveals the true nature of God and of religion." This calls every Christian church to a deep and communal examination of conscience about our fidelity, both in preaching and in practice, to the doctrines we profess to believe.

In the light of all this, four recent popes have been calling for a "new evangelization." Pope Paul VI wrote, "The Church exists to evangelize." But this can only be done through lives that provide *public and convincing proof* of the *interior transformation* promised by the Good News of "the grace of our Lord Jesus Christ."

Paul VI focused on *witness*:

Above all the Gospel must be proclaimed by witness....The first means of evangelization is the witness of an authentically

Christian life. Modern people listen more willingly to witnesses than to teachers, and if they do listen to teachers, it is because they are *witnesses*.....It is therefore primarily *by her conduct and by her life* that the Church will evangelize the world....[3]

A LIFESTYLE THAT RAISES EYEBROWS

We don't need a pope to tell us this. It is self-evident. But Paul takes us a step further into a clarity so inescapable it is daunting. Christian witness requires us to live a *lifestyle that raises eyebrows*, one that, in its own way, is just as radically arresting as the sackcloth and ashes of public penitents in the early Church.

> Above all the Gospel must be proclaimed by witness. Take a Christian or a handful of Christians who, in the midst of their own community, show their capacity for understanding and acceptance, their sharing of life and destiny with other people, their solidarity with the efforts of all for whatever is noble and good. Let us suppose that, in addition, they radiate in an altogether simple and unaffected way their faith in values that *go beyond current values*, and their hope in *something that is not seen* and that one would not dare to imagine. Through this wordless witness these Christians *stir up irresistible questions* in the hearts of those who see how they live: Why are they like this? Why do they live in this way? What or who is it that inspires them? Why are they in our midst? Such a witness is already a silent proclamation of the Good News.[4]

What we should be confronting in Confession is the sincerity — and practical demonstration — of our concern to give this kind of witness.

We are accustomed to limit our examination of conscience to sins that any human being who lives an examined life should recognize as wrong. We evaluate our lives for the most part as if we had never heard of Jesus Christ or read his Gospel. We practice a pagan morality.[5]

Does that sound harsh? Ask yourself this question: Suppose you stopped believing in Jesus Christ today. Can you name five concrete choices you would make *right now* that would significantly change your lifestyle?

Be precise. You have only stopped believing in Jesus. You still believe in God and his commandments. This is so basic to human nature that St. Paul expects it even of "good pagans."

> For what can be known about God is plain to them, because God has shown it to them. Ever since the creation of the world his eternal power and divine nature, invisible though they are, have been understood and seen through the things he has made.

Look around you. How many do you see who, although they profess no belief in Christianity, put many Christians to shame through the uprightness and generosity of their lives?

You still acknowledge and worship God. So you would not do any of the things Paul condemns in those who don't:

> Since they did not see fit to acknowledge God, God gave them up to a debased mind and to things that should not be done. They were filled with every kind of wickedness, evil, covetousness, malice. Full of envy, murder, strife, deceit, craftiness, they are gossips, slanderers, God-haters, insolent, haughty, boastful, inventors of evil, rebellious toward parents, foolish, faithless, heartless, ruthless. (Romans 1:18–32)

In other words, you would not start committing any of the sins that are listed in the standard examinations of conscience designed to help people prepare for Confession. So if you stopped believing in Jesus, *what concrete choices would you make as a result that would be visible in your lifestyle?* If you stopped believing in Jesus, who would notice? How significantly different would your behavior be?

If you cannot think of any significant changes you would make in your way of living just because you no longer believe in Jesus, what is there in your lifestyle right now that gives proof positive you do?

THE PATTERN OF EVANGELIZATION

In the first or *kerygmatic* ("heralding") preaching of the Good News as reported in the Acts of the Apostles, there is a clear pattern. First there was *an event that shocked* — something that raised questions. The disciples rushed out of the upper room on Pentecost so excited that people thought they were drunk. Later, Peter and John healed a man lame from birth, and the bystanders were astounded.

Only Scripture could provide the answers to the questions raised. Peter responded to the scoffers at Pentecost, "These men are not drunk, as you suppose, for it is only nine o'clock in the morning!" The only explanation was that Joel's prophecy was fulfilled: "I will pour out my Spirit upon all flesh, and your sons and your daughters shall prophesy." Because Jesus was risen from the dead, "having received from the Father the promise of the Holy Spirit, he has poured out this that you both see and hear."

To those who were "utterly astonished" by the cure of the lame man, Peter said, "Why do you wonder at this...as though by our own power or piety we had made him walk?...The faith that is through Jesus has given him this perfect health in the presence of all of you" (Acts 2:4–24; 3:1–16).

Evangelization depends on the *pre-evangelization* that happens because of some visible event that raises irresistible questions in people's minds that can only be answered by the presence and power of the risen Jesus acting in those upon whom his Spirit has been poured out. That visible event has to be our lifestyle.

To cut to the heart of the matter, in order to bear credible witness to Jesus — and this is a fundamental Christian obligation that should be addressed in Confession — our lifestyle has to be a visible sign and proof that Jesus has risen from the dead.

Anointed to be a sign

Jesus said the only "sign" people can expect today in support of the Gospel is the "sign of Jonah."

> No sign will be given...except the sign of the prophet Jonah. For just as Jonah was three days and three nights in the belly of the sea monster, so for three days and three nights the Son of Man will be in the heart of the earth. (Matthew 12:39–40)

Jesus' resurrection was a sign to those who with their own eyes saw him risen from the dead (1 Corinthians 15:3–9). But a sign has to be visible. So we have to say that Christ's resurrection two thousand years ago is a sign to people now because the risen Jesus lives and is visible today in those who are his body on earth. We, the Church, are the "sign of Jonah" in our time. We are the risen Jesus.

For the risen Jesus to be revealed in us, however, we have to live visibly in a way that can only be explained by the presence and power of his Spirit within us. If our lifestyle can be explained without Jesus, then Jesus is not visible in our lifestyle. And if Jesus is not visible in our lifestyle, we are failing to live up to the words of our baptismal anointing as *prophets*: "As Christ was anointed Priest, *Prophet,* and King, so live always as a member of his body." By that anointing we were committed to bear witness in the world. Whether and how we do that is matter for Confession.

If this sounds radical, it is. But a radical response is required because of the radical damage done to people's faith in our times by the mediocrity of Christians. As a Church we need to do penance for our failure to profess the Gospel credibly in action. We need to do this by engaging in actions now that are simply not credible without the Gospel.

A NEW STANDARD OF MORALITY

No official voice in the Church has been more outspoken about this than John Paul II. He has given a new and radical meaning to the word "morality."

We used to call "immoral" only those actions that were positively "bad" in some way — the kind of behavior Saint Paul said even the pagans knew enough to avoid. But John Paul changed the standard. More precisely, he recognized and publicly declared that Jesus himself changed the standard of morality for Christians when he proclaimed his New Law. We have just not noticed it or taken it seriously:

Jesus' way of acting and his words, his deeds and his precepts constitute *the moral rule* of Christian life....Christ's example, no less than his words, is *normative* for Christians.

John Paul gives concrete examples which, if we pause to read them closely, are so challenging they shock us:

The invitation, "go, sell your possessions and give the money to the poor," and the promise "you will have treasure in heaven," are *meant for everyone*, because they bring out the full meaning of the commandment of love for neighbor....["Sell all and give to the poor" means that in all our dealings with others, all we have and do should be dedicated to helping and serving them.]

"Following Christ" is not an outward imitation, since it *touches humans at the very depths of their being*. Being a follower of Christ means "becoming *conformed to him*" who became a servant even to giving himself on the cross.

The Gospel invites believers *not to accumulate* the goods of this passing world...This is a duty *intrinsic to the Christian vocation*, no less than the duty of working to overcome poverty....Those who are poor in the Gospel sense are *ready to sacrifice their resources and their own selves so that others may live*....Moderation and simplicity ought to *become the criteria of our daily lives*....

We are *obliged to support the poor* and *not just from our surplus.... Money ought not to be used for war*, nor for destroying and killing, but for defending the dignity of human beings, for improving their life and for building a truly open, free and harmonious society....[6]

He goes further than this. John Paul at first appears to accept the right to kill in self-defense or in "just" wars. But if we read him closely, his real teaching seems to be that we must renounce that right in order to be fully Christian.

Taking up explicitly the doctrine of the cross as taught and modeled by Jesus, he affirms that for Christians life "finds its... meaning and its fulfillment when it is given up" in love for others; that we are called "to give our lives for our brothers and sisters, and thus to realize in the fullness of truth the meaning and destiny of our existence." To renounce the right to self-defense, he tells us, is an act of "heroic love which deepens and transfigures the love of self into a radical self-offering, according to the spirit of the Gospel Beatitudes (cf. Matthew 5:38–40). The sublime example of this self-offering is the Lord Jesus himself."

Since John Paul has proclaimed repeatedly that "Jesus' way of acting and his words, his deeds and his precepts *constitute the moral rule of Christian life,*" and that "Christ's example, no less than his words, *is normative for Christians,*" he is obviously proposing this heroic love as the normal standard of virtue that Christians should strive to embrace. The Christian vocation is to give oneself in perfect love for others, and Jesus made clear what that love calls us to do: "No one has greater love than this, to lay down one's life for one's friends."[7]

No one is obliged to accept John Paul's teaching about this. Even Catholics are free to disagree with it, and in practice many do. *But no Christian is free to deny the obligation of bearing radical witness to Jesus Christ in this world by living in a way that makes his presence in them an undeniable proof of his resurrection and of the gift of the Spirit.*

Not to confront these radical challenges is, for Christians, to live "an unexamined life." If we do not examine our lives in the light of the radical call of the Gospel, it is not our Christian life that we are examining.

GETTING DOWN TO PRACTICE

We will consider later what questions we should ask when we are preparing for Confession. Here we just want to look at some questions we should not fail to ask.

We should remember that the New Testament word for "sin" is *hamartia,* which literally means to "miss" or "fall short." It is not enough to ask what we are doing that is positively wrong. We have to ask how we are falling short of authentic Christian living. To live up to our baptismal commitment as prophet we have to change our whole standard of morality. Once we accept to be prophets we never ask again just whether something is right or wrong — we ask, "How does this bear witness to the values of Jesus Christ?"

We are committed by Baptism and by love itself to bear witness to the Good News of Jesus. We cannot do this effectively unless our lifestyle raises "irresistible questions" in people's minds that can only be answered by the Gospel. Therefore, we need to confront in Confession what there is in our lifestyle that is so visibly, obviously — even shockingly — different from the ordinary "good behavior" of upright people that it challenges basic assumptions and values in our peer group. What are we doing that raises eyebrows?

We cannot even begin to do this unless we are *disciples* — that is, "students" of the mind and heart of God as revealed in the Scriptures. Without personal reflection on the words and example of Jesus, we will have no standard to judge ourselves by except the "law," which in practice means the rules and practices taken for granted in our religion. At best this is dependence on someone else's experience of the Holy Spirit, not our own. At worst it is simply religious conformism (the scriptural name for this is *Phariseeism*). To be a Pharisee, you don't have to be a hypocrite; you just have to reduce your religion to observance of all the rules.

As disciples and prophets, Christians measure their behavior by its conformity to the words and example of Jesus — absorbed through personal reflection enlightened by the gift of the Holy Spirit. In this there is always "forward motion." To live that "life to the full" that Jesus came to give requires unending *metanoia,* an ongoing "change of mind" (the Gospel call to "repent"). This engages us in continual *conversion* — that is, in continual *change* of attitudes, values, and behavior.

If we accept our baptismal anointing as prophets, then we should think about confessing our *conversions* instead of focusing only on our "sins." What have I seen in the Scriptures since my last Confession that is calling me to more? What movements of grace have I experienced, and how have I responded to them? What have I "changed my mind" about? What *changes* have I made in my lifestyle that make it more reflective of the Good News? Am I raising any eyebrows where I live and work and socialize? Has anybody asked me any questions? Do some people shy away from me because I am a threat to their complacency, to their own conformity to the peer group? Have I myself accepted to "fit in"?

The gift of the Spirit

In the early Church it was taken for granted that Baptism should be accompanied or followed by the "gift of the Holy Spirit."[8] So if I accept that, as an anointed *prophet,* I have been given the "gift of the Spirit," then I should expect to be hearing his voice.

The Spirit, however, seldom shouts. His inspirations usually take the form of a non-intrusive thought, a hardly recognized impulse to take some action, a recurring doubt about a decision we have never really looked at. If we are not actively trying to "hear his voice" and "discern what is the will of God — what is good and acceptable and perfect" (Hebrews 3:7; Romans 12:2), these inspirations will probably go unnoticed. But if we ask ourselves, in preparation for Confession, what thoughts or feelings we have failed to focus on that may have been inspirations of the Holy Spirit, we can gradually grow into familiarity with his voice.

To recognize the gift of the Spirit is also a mystical experience. Where do we seek this recognition?

Within the overall gift of the Spirit, Christian tradition, inspired by Isaiah's prophecy about the Messiah (11:2–3), has focused on seven particular "gifts of the Spirit." Four are gifts that raise the operations of the intellect to a divine level: *wisdom, understanding, knowledge,* and *counsel.* Three support the will: *piety, fortitude,* and *fear of the Lord.*[9]

We could get in touch with the gift of the Spirit by examining our experience of each particular gift. Have we been given a taste for spiritual things (*wisdom,* from *sapientia, sapor,* or, in English, "savor")? Which truths of the faith are especially clear and evident to us, enough to be motivating in our lives (*understanding*)? What practical "know-how" (*knowledge*) have we acquired in living the spiritual life? In particularly difficult decisions, have we recognized help (*counsel*) received from the Holy Spirit as Paraclete — Advocate or "lawyer"?

In our daily dealing with others, are we animated by the family spirit of love and loyalty that is the true meaning of *piety*? When we shrink from what is difficult or threatening, have we found strength in *fortitude* given by the Spirit? And has *fear of the Lord* held us back from yielding to the dangerous attraction of riches, honors, and pleasure?

It would be helpful to prepare for Confession by asking about our use and experience of these gifts.

THE FRUIT OF THE SPIRIT

Even more helpful, perhaps, is to ask whether or not our life is characterized by the "fruit of the Spirit" as Paul describes it in Galatians (5:22–23). "The fruit of the Spirit is *love, joy, peace, patient endurance, kindness, generosity, faithfulness, gentleness, and self-control.*"

When people in business want to examine how they are doing, they do not first get out their Business Administration textbooks and look for what rules they might be breaking. Their first act is to look at the bottom line: is it red or black? Are they making money or losing it? If they are losing money, they look for what is causing that. Then they might look at the textbooks.

When we examine our spiritual lives, it doesn't make sense to start by asking what rules we are breaking. We may find some, but more than likely we have already rationalized the root problems, the attitudes, values, and behavior that are doing real damage to ourselves and others. As we will see again in a later chapter, the sins that do the most harm are seldom, if ever, brought to Confession.

When people get divorced, it is almost certain that the real cause is something that was never dealt with — or even thought of — in Confession. When people stop showing up on Sundays, leave the Church, or lose the faith, this is not the result of any sins they have confessed. It is the result of the sins they did not confess because they never recognized them as sins. Whatever they were doing that was killing their faith, they never acknowledged it as sin.

An obvious example is young people who stop going to church because it "never meant anything." Of course it didn't. They were not really "meaning" anything they said or sang in church. They were just being borne along by the crowd, more passively than actively. They did not come to church with the intention of praising God, thanking God, celebrating the mystery of God's action in the world with conscious focus. During the readings and preaching on Scripture they just sat back like an audience, waiting for something to "turn them on." They were not there as *disciples*, actively intent on learning something from the word of God.

If they were bored during the Eucharistic Prayer, it was because they were not paying attention to the words. The words are exciting — if we listen for the mystery they express.

When (and if) they went to Confession, they did not confess "not getting into" the Mass. Or not praising God. Or not thanking him. They never asked themselves whether the life of grace was dying within them because they were failing to nurture it. They just confessed some obvious faults that had little to do with their real failure to "do the will of God from the heart" (Ephesians 6:6). The sins that nudged them out of the Church were never brought to the Church for healing, advice, or conversion. Obviously, they were never taught to use Confession as they should.

Suppose we changed our starting point. Suppose we began to prepare for Confession by asking, "Is my life *characterized* by love? Am I habitually filled with deep *joy*? Do I live with an abiding sense of *peace*?"

If the answer is "Yes," then I am experiencing the first three realities Paul describes as the "fruit of the Spirit." If the fruit of the Spirit is present in my life, then I must be living the life of the Spirit. If the fruit is not there...well, Jesus said, "By their fruits you will know them" (Matthew 7:15–20).

An effective way to examine your conscience before Confession is to forget all about your conscience, which is not always that trustworthy. Instead, ask whether Christianity is bearing in your life the fruit Jesus promised it would. If it is not, the fault does not lie with Jesus. Neither can we blame it all on the shortcomings of our parents, peer group, priests, teachers, and pastoral ministers. We all received the "gift of the Spirit" at Baptism. If that gift is not bearing its fruit in our lives, then something is wrong inside of us. And we need to find it.

Why is my life not characterized by love? By joy? By peace? By patient endurance, kindness, generosity, faithfulness, gentleness, and self-control? When I find the answers to those questions, I will know what to bring to Confession.

Jesus said, "Ask, and it will be given you; seek, and you will find; knock, and the door will be opened for you." Is there any reason to believe he will not keep that promise when we prepare for Confession? Provided, of course, that we persevere in asking the right questions and trying to be open to the answers.

When Confession calls us to ask the questions we need to ask, we will feel the Holy Spirit calling us beyond law-observance to spiritual response; beyond good behavior to witness; beyond legalism to discernment. This is to experience the "gift of the Spirit." Then Confession becomes "the sacrament of the Spirit."

CHAPTER FOUR

The Sacrament *of the* Flesh

Experiencing the priesthood of Baptism

When I was growing up in four-percent-Catholic Dallas, the Protestants, including my Baptist father, used to ask, "Why do you have to confess your sins to a man?"

My father knew the Catholic answer. He just wanted to be sure his sons did. But we Catholics asked the question ourselves. And the answer we got from the priests and nuns was unfortunately an answer to the question as it was asked: "Why do you *have* to...?"

The real question should have been, "Why do you *get* to...?" What do you get out of confessing your sins to another human being? What is the point, and what are the advantages? For us at the time there was only one advantage. We Catholics had a guaranteed, certified assurance from God that the sins we confessed were forgiven.

It should be perfectly obvious to everyone that God forgives anyone and everyone who repents of sin, as soon as, if not before, we ask. But several generations of Catholics before the Second Vatican Council were given the impression, in the common, very basic catechetical teaching they received, that anyone who sinned had to confess those sins to a priest in the sacrament of Confession (now called "Reconciliation") to be forgiven.

This was not absolute. Even in fifth grade we knew (because Sister Celeste taught us) that if we made an "act of perfect contrition" we were forgiven without Confession — although we were obliged by Church law to confess to a priest as soon as possible after that. But the "act" (prayer, profession, statement to God) of "perfect contrition" was presented as something so perfect that none of us, especially the boys, could have made one with a blueprint. So to be safe, if we committed any sin that was serious, we had better get to Confession as soon as the church doors opened, or we might get hit by a truck, die, and spend all of eternity in Hell.

It was a pretty good sales pitch for Confession. On Saturday nights we lined up — children, adolescents, and adults — outside the two confessionals in our parish church to "get absolution" and have our sins forgiven. We were glad we could do it, grateful for the guarantee, for the sacrament that gave us assurance that, whatever we had done, for the time being we were "safe" from God — at least until we did it the next time. For us, the purpose of Confession was very clear: it was fire insurance.

We knew that the Baptists and even the Hindus could be saved (by something called "Baptism of desire") and that the

Baptists thought they already were, no matter what sins they continued to commit. But to us that seemed a pretty risky proposition. We Catholics could hear it from the lips of God himself, speaking through the lips of the priest, "Go in peace, your sins are forgiven." The difficulty of actually telling our sins to the priest was a small price to pay for that reassurance.

In our mentality at the time, the only thing we cared about in Confession was "getting absolution." As adolescents we did not know that the vast majority of adults were really using Confession as a sort of spiritual "progress report" that kept them conscious of what God asked of them and constant in trying to live up to it. I'm sure they weren't even really aware that that's what they were doing; I didn't discover it until much later, when hearing confessions as a priest. But it seemed clear that for most, Confession was already an "expression of concern" to be authentic Christians, giving an integral response to the call of the Gospel — but not much was said about this in preaching and teaching. People went to Confession for many reasons and got all sorts of benefits from it, but what they were consciously focused on was simply getting absolution.

EXPERIENCING THE INCARNATION

Imperfect as that understanding may be, let's not dismiss the benefits of absolution too quickly. In receiving absolution those who came to Confession were having an experience of God. And in particular, of God incarnate, God made flesh in Jesus Christ.

Go back in time. See yourself in Jerusalem, standing in a crowd, listening to Jesus preach. You are weighed down by some really terrible sin you have committed, and guilt is eating you up. You know from the prophets that God forgives:

> Come...says the LORD: though your sins are like scarlet,
> they shall be like snow; though they are red like crimson,
> they shall become like wool. (Isaiah 1:18)

But still you feel doubt. You believe and you don't dare to believe. You feel some reassurance, but you don't feel really embraced.

You have heard about the way Jesus responded to the woman caught in the act of adultery, and how he accepted the Samaritan woman who had lived with five husbands and now was living with a man who was not her husband: how Jesus asked her to give him a drink, struck up a conversation with her, and used her to bring her whole town to himself. You have listened to him tell the story of the Prodigal Son and heard him cry out the invitation: "*Come to me*, all you that are weary and are carrying heavy burdens, and I will give you rest" (John 4:18; 8:1–11; Luke 15:11–32;Matthew 11:28). You have been deeply moved by the evident love and mercy in his heart.

Then the preaching is over, the crowd disperses, and you find yourself alone with Jesus. Just the two of you. What would you do?

You have already "confessed your sin to God." But now the incarnate God is standing before you in the flesh, able to speak with human words, to reach out and touch with human hands. You don't know enough to say in words, "This is God," because that has not yet been completely revealed. But you know in some way that in Jesus it is God you are dealing with, that Jesus speaks for God and God speaks in him. What would you do? What would you like to do?

Wouldn't it make a difference if you could go up to Jesus, tell him your sin, pour out your heart to him, feel him reach out and touch you in response, and hear him saying to you with a human voice full of love and compassion, "Your sins are forgiven. Go in peace"?

That is what Confession is.

A DIVINE-HUMAN ENCOUNTER

A sacrament is an interaction with God embodied in interaction with human beings. In sacramental interactions, the human being we interact with must be someone who has "become Christ" through Baptism, someone who is the living body of Jesus on earth. Someone in whom Jesus himself can listen and speak and touch.[1]

What we experience in Confession is an interaction that is fully human in all it involves. On the part of the one confiding, Confession is a human expression of trust embodied in a real act of self-revelation, with all the risk and vulnerability that includes. Confession is an act of faith and trust in God that is experienced as real because it is embodied in a human interaction with another human being.

There is no real act of self-revelation when we confess our sins to God — God already knows them. The risk, the vulnerability, and therefore the experience of love and trust comes through sacramental Confession, because we are exposing ourselves to someone who does not know our sins. That is what makes it human. But we are doing so as an expression and experience of love and trust in God. That is what makes it divine.

When we confess our sins to another human being, accepting that person as Jesus embodied and acting on earth, we confess to the incarnate God in an interaction that is both human and divine. It is our human interaction with God, the two of us speaking and acting in a physical body, through human words and gestures, that makes our confession "sacramental." This also makes it specifically *Christian*, because Christianity is precisely and uniquely the religion of divine-human interaction with God *made flesh* in Jesus Christ. Before Jesus came, God forgave everybody who asked him to. Now, in addition to this, he forgives through human interaction with Jesus alive, present, and acting in his body on earth. That is the special value of sacramental absolution.

Confession gives relief. It is as simple as that. A Protestant woman in Memphis, Tennessee, who made use of Confession emailed me:

> My manager asked me why the "confession" thing — and I told him that it's the most wonderful thing around. I know I've sinned, and I know the Lord knows it — but when I acknowledge it to him — and he does his thing with it — it's like emptying out my "backpack"....lightens the load tremendously, and I can be happy again — secure in knowing that he loves me still.

During retreats I have directed, I have occasionally encountered people who confess some sin they have never revealed, even though for twenty years or more they have been using Confession regularly. It isn't that they were making dishonest or "bad" confessions: they may have been rationalizing, or confessing the sin in a way so vague and general they knew the priest would not understand. Or they may have just never found a confessor they felt would be compassionate enough for them to risk revealing this particular sin. And they trusted in God to understand that. But in the experience of the retreat, when they were able to get a "feel" for how the confessor would react, they decided to unburden themselves.

And it was exactly that. It was like lancing a boil. They felt a relief and peace that had been missing for twenty years. What made the difference was confessing to God present and listening, present and responding, in another human being.

Confession is an experience — and if we engage in it with conscious faith, let's not hesitate to call it a mystical experience — of Jesus Christ loving us and expressing his love in human words of forgiveness and acceptance. It is the sacrament of forgiveness *enfleshed*.

CONFESSION AND COUNSELING

Confession also includes counseling. This may or may not be significant in a given case, but there is great value in having someone always available for consultation about problems and questions that arise in our spiritual life.

Think of teenagers. They know that if they ever do anything they are afraid to talk about, even with their parents, there is an adult always available in the confessional, one who presumably has some wisdom. He is there at fixed times; there is no need to make an appointment, and the "reconciliation room" is set up so they can talk either anonymously or face-to-face, whatever makes them more comfortable. They know that the priest cannot reveal what he hears in the confessional, even to save lives. The "seal of confession" is absolute. Nothing takes priority over it, and there are no exceptions. This gives the teenager someone to talk to.

A side effect of this absolute secrecy is that even the smallest child is made aware that sin is first and foremost an interaction between oneself and God. The secrecy of Confession is protected by the strictest laws and sanctions of the Church. This says that the Church sees Confession as a sacrament that is so important for the removal of personal guilt, and for the restoration of personal peace in relationship to God, that no fear of exposure, for any reason at all, can be allowed to block anyone from making use of it. I grew up knowing from earliest childhood that if I confessed to a priest, "I put a bomb in the church," and if there was no way he could defuse the bomb or warn those present without revealing that I had put it there, he would just have to let the whole congregation be blown up and die along with them. (I realized later that this was a pretty hypothetical "if.") Because of the absolute secrecy of the confessional, I knew, before I had ever heard the word, that both Confession and sin have a "transcendent" dimension. They both concern primarily my relationship with the Infinite God.

If my right to confess my sin to God through the priest is so important that the fear of exposure must never be allowed, under any circumstances, to be an impediment to it, then what is being protected is my right to deal with God himself in Confession. Implicit in this is the realization that, if forgiveness of sin is essentially an act of God, then every sin is also essentially an offense against God. This gives sin a dimension that is clearly beyond mere failure in our duty to other human beings. It is more than just not being "nice."

My first conscious experience of personal relationship with God came when I was less than five years old. I was angry with my brother, a year older than I. To taunt me, he was holding

up one object after another, which I would spit at. Finally he
held up a crucifix. Without thinking, I spit at that too. Then
my brother gleefully cried, "That's a mortal sin! You're going to
Hell!"

Even then I knew there was something wrong with his logic
and that I had not committed a "mortal sin." But just confronting the question made me very deeply aware — for the
first time — that Someone was present who was aware of my
actions. And I knew that I was accountable to him, not just
to other people and parents. I think that was my entry into
personal relationship with God and conscious awareness of
my belief in God, even though I could not have used either of
those expressions at the time.

This side trip into the "collateral benefit" of confessional secrecy circles back into the confessor's role as counselor. His job,
besides answering questions, is to help the confider understand
the experience of enlightenment — of faith, hope, and love —
that is taking place in the confrontation and confession of sins.
Sometimes this includes commonsense human advice as well.

There is, however, a big difference between sacramental
Confession and psychological counseling. What is primary
in Confession is the recognized action of God (although
Christian psychologists also rely implicitly on his action in
them). But even for spiritual discernment, confessors need to
be humanly as well as spiritually qualified. Otherwise, God
would have to turn ministry into magic. John Paul II sets the
bar pretty high for those human qualifications:

> For the effective performance of this ministry, the confessor
> must necessarily have human qualities of prudence, discre-
> tion, discernment and a firmness tempered by gentleness
> and kindness. He must likewise have a serious and careful

preparation, not fragmentary but complete and harmonious, in the different branches of theology, pedagogy and psychology, in the methodology of dialogue and above all in a living and communicable knowledge of the word of God. But it is even more necessary that he should live an intense and genuine spiritual life. In order to lead others along the path of Christian perfection the minister of penance himself must first travel this path.[2]

If Confession is to be experienced as what it really is, a lot is required of the confessor. Admittedly, this is not always present. That risk is what makes Confession a real and very human act of faith and trust in God, an act of vulnerable self-exposure. When Confession is what is should be, it is an experience of encounter with the God of steadfast love responding in the body of the living, loving Christ to the sins and failures, the weakness and need, and above all, to the faith, confidence, and love that are receiving expression in the confession of sins. Ideally, confessors should respond to what they hear with the compassion and love of Jesus himself. That is what they are there for. And normally, that is what happens.

THE EXPERIENCE OF PRIESTHOOD

When I first began hearing confessions as a young priest, my strongest impression was, "I am loving above my head." The expression came from the athletic slang of the day: a team was "playing above its head" when they were performing better than their experience told them they were able to perform. And I knew in the confessional that I was responding to what

I heard with a love that was not my own — or was my own only because I was sharing in and expressing the love of Jesus Christ living in me. Confessors, being human, might react in all sorts of negative ways to things done around — or especially to — them in daily life. But when they are in that confessional, they know (or should know, and most of them do) that they are there to respond as Jesus, and only as Jesus, to anything and everything they hear. And they find they are empowered to do this.

For the confessor too, Confession is a mystical experience. If it is not a mystical experience, both for the confider and the confessor, one or both are failing to do what they should do. The mystical experience of Confession, both for the confessor and the confider, is an experience of the *priesthood* given in Baptism.

Those confessing their sins experience the ministry of Jesus giving them life through the priesthood of the confessor. They experience Jesus expressing his divine love for them in and through the human expression of the minister who is his body. This is both healing and life-giving.

But this experience segues into the experience of Jesus giving life to others in and through the priesthood that those who seek Confession themselves have received as "priests in the Priest" by Baptism. This is a natural consequence, one only to be expected in people called and committed to live out Jesus' "new commandment": "Love one another *as I have loved you.*" In Christianity, what we receive we give. What we receive as fruit from branches united to the vine is the fruit we give to others as branches of the same vine. It is all one constant, two-way experience of receiving and giving as people who share in the priesthood of God-made-flesh in Jesus, the one and only Priest who endures.[3]

The exercise of priesthood is the mediation of divine life through its human expression in the flesh. The experience of ministry as a priest is union with God experienced in surrender to God's desire to speak and act in and through one's body. When Jesus said, "It is more blessed to give than to receive," he may have had this mystical experience in mind (Acts 20:35).

THE COMMISSION TO EXPRESS

This leads us to add another focus to our examination of conscience. Have we been faithful to our baptismal consecration as *priests*? By the words of our baptismal anointing, "As Christ was anointed *Priest, Prophet, and King,* so live as a member of his body," we were solemnly and explicitly committed, not just to love, but to *express* it.

It should be obvious that the sins we need to be most aware of are our failures to love. Jesus declared unambiguously that the "first and greatest" commandment is to love God with our whole heart and soul and mind and strength. And the second is to love "our neighbor as ourselves" (Mark 12:28–31). It should, then, be instilled in us by all the religious formation we receive, from childhood to death, that as Christians we wake up to love, spend our day giving love, and go to sleep asking ourselves whether we have, in fact, been loving to every person we have encountered.

Jesus, however, changed the "second greatest" commandment.

When asked, "Who is my neighbor?" he told the story of the Good Samaritan. A priest and a Levite, both members of the priestly caste, pass by a Jew left for dead by robbers. But he is helped by a Samaritan, one of a group whom the Jews ostracized as heretics and foreigners. When Jesus asked which of the three people in his story — the priest, the Levite, or the foreigner — "was a neighbor to the man who fell into the hands of the robbers," he evoked the answer: "The one who showed him mercy" (Luke 10:25–37). By drawing the conclusion "Go and do likewise," Jesus changed the meaning both of "neighbor" and of "mercy."

The root meaning of "mercy" is "to come to the aid of another out of a sense of *relationship*." It carries the same weight as the foundational virtue of Roman culture — the *pietas* of *pius Aeneas* in the *Aeneid* — which meant loyalty to family, friends, and fellow citizens, to the gods of hearth and homeland. In Spanish, "Have mercy" is translated "*Ten piedad.*" When Jesus taught us to "have mercy" on everyone in need, he extended *pietas* and "love of neighbor" to embrace the whole human race.

He went even farther than this. At the Last Supper he said, "I give you a *new* commandment, that you love one another... *as I have loved you*" (John 13:34; 15:12). This commits us to love beyond all bounds, to love with the dimensions, the "breadth and length and height and depth," of Christ's own love "that surpasses knowledge," so that we may be filled and fill the whole world "with all the fullness of God" (Ephesians 3:18–19).

How, in one word, did Jesus love us? He loved us by *expressing* his love, God's love, in the flesh. This is the key to the Incarnation and to John's Gospel:

> In the beginning was the Word, and the Word was with God, and the Word was God....In him was life, and the life was the light of all people....And the Word became flesh and lived among us, and we have *seen his glory*...full of grace and truth....

No one has ever seen God. It is God the only Son, who is close to the Father's heart, who has made him known.

Jesus was the revelation, the expression in the flesh, of God's steadfast love.[4]

Jesus showed his love by expressing it in physical words and actions, culminating in the most passionate physical expression of love ever given in the history of the world, his self-oblation on the cross. John says, "The way we came to know love was that he laid down his life for us." And so, to love each other as he loved us, "we ought to lay down our lives for one another" (1 John 3:16).

How do we do this? Not by literally dying, but by the "daily dying" to self, which consists in offering our bodies as a "living sacrifice" to God in every interaction we have with other human beings (Romans 12:1). We do this in practice by using our *bodies* as the medium through which we mediate the divine life of God to others by letting the invisible life of God within us *express* itself in visible manifestations of faith, hope, and love.

We smile at people. Without being explicit about it, we treat them as brothers and sisters in Christ. We have no "purely professional" or functional encounters: in every interaction we make it clear that we see, respect, and acknowledge every person's humanity, every person's feelings, every person's value and dignity as equal to our own, even as divine. To show love is to affirm relationship, whether explicitly or implicitly. It is not enough to love in our hearts, or to think loving thoughts. To communicate the love of God to others as *priests* we have to express it. That is what God did by becoming flesh in Jesus Christ.

So the mystical experience of priesthood, received both in ministering and in being ministered to, is an experience of Jesus living and loving, healing and enhancing, through the physical, visible, audible words and actions of his body on earth. It is the experience both of finding and of being — an *enfleshed encounter with God.*

The physical encounter with Jesus in Confession is one of the most powerful ways available to experience this. Confessing regularly our successes and failures in giving expression to his love is an effective way to make this experience a habit.

CHAPTER FIVE

The Sacrament *of* Stewardship

Experiencing the giftedness of accountability
Acknowledging responsibility for the reign
of God

I t is true that every sin is an individual act of free choice, involving individual, personal guilt. But it can be argued that this is not the predominate viewpoint in Scripture.

We tend to forget that the Ten Commandments were not given to us as individuals, but to a people — who by accepting them became the People of God (Exodus 1:1—20:17; 24:1–8). To observe the Commandments was to keep the Covenant. It was not just religion; it was the most basic, important act of patriotism. The common good of the community depended on everyone's keeping up the People's end of the bargain. And thus, we have the communal dimension of Confession: it is always an act of reconciliation with the community. The individual is reconciled into the harmony of the community, and the community is restored by the reconciliation.

What God promised, as his side of the Covenant, was not just individual salvation. It was to bring the People into the Promised Land and preserve them as long as they were faithful. That is why those who sinned were accountable to the whole community. By breaking the Covenant they endangered the promise that was the common good of all. They put the whole People in the way of disaster.

When Jesus gave his New Law, and specifically his "new commandment," it was in the context of entering into a New Covenant with his people.

> I give you a new commandment, that you love one another. Just as I have loved you, you also should love one another. By this everyone will know that you are my disciples, if you have love for one another. (John 13:34–35)

> Then he took a loaf of bread, and when he had given thanks, he broke it and gave it to them, saying, "This is my body, which is given for you. Do this in remembrance of me." And he did the same with the cup after supper, saying, "This cup that is poured out for you is the new covenant in my blood." (Luke 22:19–20)

We keep the law of Christ, not just because we are humans, but because we are *Christians*. By entering into the Church, we entered into a new covenant with God. That covenant commits us to abide by his words and unites us to all who are likewise committed and redeemed by his blood. If we fail to live up to it, we are failing not only Jesus but also our brothers and sisters in the new People of God.

THE KINGDOM: PROMISE AND COMMITMENT

What Jesus promises in the new Covenant is not just individual salvation, as some kind of private enjoyment of God. Jesus promises to bring those who are faithful to the new Covenant into the new Promised Land, the Kingdom of God.

> From that time Jesus began to proclaim, "Repent, for the kingdom of heaven has come near."
>
> "Blessed are the poor in spirit, for theirs is the kingdom of heaven."
>
> "For I tell you, unless your righteousness exceeds that of the scribes and Pharisees, you will never enter the kingdom of heaven" (Matthew 4:17; 5:3, 20).

That is why Christians who sin today are also accountable to the whole community. By breaking the new Covenant we delay the coming of the Kingdom of God, which is the common good, not only of the People of God, but of the whole human race.

But there is more. At Baptism every single Christian was given a special responsibility through the solemn anointing that made us *stewards* of the Kingship of Christ. The mission of the Church is to work for the establishment of God's reign over every area and activity of human life on earth. That is what it means to establish the Kingdom. We were consecrated and committed by Baptism to take responsibility for this as "kings" or stewards of Christ's Kingship, and to assume leadership in bringing it about.

The words of our anointing were, "As Christ was anointed

Priest, Prophet, and King, so live always as a member of his body."

Confession, if we choose to make full use of it, can be for us a preview and preparation for the day when we will be called to "give an account of our stewardship" (Luke 16:2). Confession provides a means to review and improve our exercise of responsible leadership in the Church and in the world.

THE ACCEPTANCE OF ACCOUNTABILITY

Jesus speaks in several places of *accountability*, especially in the context of stewardship.

We are accountable, first of all, for our personal lives: "I tell you, on the day of judgment you will have to give an account for every careless word you utter" (Matthew 12:36, and read all of the "Sermon on the Mount," chapters 5 to 7).

Because we are rational beings, created in the image of God, our stewardship includes both dominion over and responsibility for everything God has created. Accountability for the environment is a basic moral imperative.

> Then God said, "Let us make humankind in our image, according to our likeness; and let them have dominion over the fish of the sea, and over the birds of the air, and over the cattle, and over all the wild animals of the earth, and over every creeping thing that creeps upon the earth." (Genesis 1:26-28)

Catholics proclaim in the Mass that we are the "stewards of creation":

> You chose to create us in your own image,

setting us over the whole world in all its wonder.
You made us the *stewards of creation*,
to praise you day by day for the marvels of your wisdom
and power,
through Jesus Christ our Lord. (Fourth Eucharistic Prayer
and Fifth Preface for Sundays)

We are especially responsible and accountable for the well-being of other human beings:

Then the LORD said to Cain, "Where is your brother Abel?"
He said, "I do not know; am I my brother's keeper?" And the
LORD said, "What have you done? Listen; your brother's
blood is crying out to me from the ground!" (Genesis 4:9–10)

It is not only the blood we ourselves have shed that cries out to God. It is all the blood that is shed on the earth, literally and figuratively, because of "man's inhumanity to man." We are required — as our brothers' and sisters' keepers — to address both the causes and the effects of all injustice and all callousness to human suffering. But as Christians we are asked even more. We are responsible for recognizing and responding to all who are "in Christ," loving them, not just as fellow members of the human race, but as true children of our common Father in grace, members of the divine body of Christ on earth, and as Christ himself:

Then they will answer, "Lord, when was it that we saw you
hungry or thirsty or a stranger or naked or sick or in prison,
and did not take care of you?" Then he will answer them,
"Truly I tell you, just as you did not do it to one of the least
of these, you did not do it to me." (Matthew 25:44-45)

As Christians we are accountable for using the gifts God has given us to contribute not just to the human well-being of others on earth, but also to their spiritual growth and development.

> You are the salt of the earth; but if salt has lost its taste, how can its saltiness be restored? It is no longer good for anything, but is thrown out and trampled under foot. You are the light of the world....No one after lighting a lamp puts it under the bushel basket, but on the lampstand, and it gives light to all in the house....Let your light shine before others, so that they may see your good works and give glory to your Father in heaven. (Matthew 5:13-16)

The gifts God has given us are an investment. He wants a return on them. He will hold us accountable, as his stewards and managers, for using them in such a way that we bear divine fruit on earth, "fruit that will endure" — the fruit of eternal life (Matthew 7:17–20; 13:23; 25:14–30; John 15:12-16; Romans 7:4).

> The Lord said, "Who then is the faithful and prudent manager whom his master will put in charge of his servants, to give them their allowance of food at the proper time? Blessed is that servant whom his master will find *at work* when he arrives." (see Luke 12:36-44)

In the words of Paul we are "servants of Christ and stewards of God's mysteries." In those of Peter we are "stewards of the manifold grace of God," charged to "serve one another with whatever gift each...has received." Paul defines the moral principle: "It is required of stewards that they be found trustworthy." (1 Corinthians 4:1–4; 1 Peter 4:10). To be a *steward* is to accept responsibility and be faithful in exercising it.

According to Paul, it is a mark of Christian maturity to take responsibility for "building up the Church." He told the Corinthians that as long as they were basking in the thrill of their charismatic gifts and coming to church just to be "turned on," they were "infants in Christ." The "manifestation of the Spirit" is given, not for personal consolation, but "for the common good."

> Brothers and sisters, do not be children in your thinking; rather, be infants in evil, but in thinking be adults. What should be done then, my friends? When you come together....let all things be done for *building up.* (1 Corinthians 3:1; 12:7; 13:11; 14:1–26)

What Paul is telling the Corinthians, and through them us, is "Grow up!" We reach maturity when we take responsibility, as stewards of Christ the King, for building up the Church and establishing the "reign of God" on earth.

> The gifts he gave were...to equip the saints for the work of ministry, for building up the body of Christ, until all of us come...to maturity....We must no longer be children...But speaking the truth in love, we must grow up in every way into him who is the head, into Christ, from whom the whole body...as each part is working properly, promotes the body's growth in building itself up in love. (Ephesians 4:11–16)

This is our responsibility, our commitment, and our baptismal consecration as *stewards* of the kingship of Christ. How we live up to it is matter we should bring to Confession.

THE SINS WE DON'T CONFESS

There is in the Catholic Church a phenomenon that may be

common to all religions — the sins that do the most damage on earth are seldom, if ever, faced in conscience or mentioned in Confession. It is not that people are deliberately refusing to admit their sins. It is just that people don't recognize some of the worst things they do as sins. In many cases they don't even have to be rationalized. Nobody ever thinks about them. When the seed of God's word challenges something that "everybody does," it falls on the beaten path of culture and never even penetrates (see Matthew 13:4).

Obvious examples from Christian history are slavery, the burning of heretics at the stake, torture of prisoners, innumerable wars of aggression fought with unrebuked savagery, racial discrimination, and socially acceptable exploitation of the poor. We can be sure none of these were ever brought to Confession!

We have come a long way, but we have an even longer way to go.

Christians have rejected slavery and today almost unanimously respect the right of religious freedom. We have made stunning progress against racial discrimination and significant progress against the exploitation of the poor. We affirm equal status for women and are raising serious questions about the death penalty and the morality of war. There has been an outcry against the government's recently sanctioned torture of prisoners.

At the same time, in most of these areas the evil is far from abolished. What we teach in theory is unknown by many and ignored by others in practice. When individuals do sin against anything in the area of "social justice," they seldom, if ever, acknowledge it as sin — certainly not in the confessional.

In 1970 I was sent as pastor to integrate two parishes in

Louisiana: one black, one white. In the two years it took to accomplish this, the question of integration came up in almost every parish meeting and discussion. There was no area of parish life in which racism was not an issue — except one: the confession of sins. In the confessional no one had a problem with racism. The sin that was threatening to destroy the parish just never came up in Confession (well, hardly ever).

With exceptions too rare to be counted, my experience in the confessional would lead me to conclude that in the Catholic Church there are no mechanics who cheat on repairs, no salesmen who lie to prospective buyers, no advertisers who "sell with sleaze," no merchants who deceive customers, no employers who pay unjust wages, no employees who don't give a full day's work for a full day's pay, no one who practices discrimination against anyone, and no doctors, lawyers, or politicians who are not totally conscientious in everything they do. No one is unduly attached to affluence or spends too much on clothes, cars, or entertainment. No women dress immodestly, and no men dress to look macho or important, including bishops. There are no career-minded, lazy, or arrogant priests. It goes without saying that you would never know from hearing confessions — whether from perpetrators or victims — that there has ever been a problem of child abuse in the clergy or in any other category of persons in the Catholic Church. And if there were cover-ups, you would have to read the newspapers to find out about them. This list could go on and on.

Those who commit the most serious sins — in any area of life — either do not come to Confession at all, or they are so brainwashed by their culture and peer group that in matters of social justice, business, and politics they don't know right from wrong.

THE CULTURAL CONSCIENCE

None of this says that Confession is a farce. That conclusion would be utterly, unjustly, and indefensibly false. In my experience, almost every single person who uses Confession is sincere and honestly trying to live an authentic Christian life. Almost all are confessing their sins as they see them. The problem is, especially in the areas of social justice, business, and politics, they don't see them.

The professor who taught us moral theology in the seminary I attended in France had been a contractor before he was a priest. He went to great lengths to explain to us the realities of the business environment in France. "The French custom," he said, "is to cheat thirty-three and a third percent on income tax. It's a national statistic. As a result, the government raises all of the income taxes by thirty-three and a third percent, right across the board. So if anyone tells you in Confession he is cheating on his income tax, you should ask, 'How much?' If he says, 'Twenty-three percent,' tell him he has ten percent to go!"

Local attitudes and customs can make moral judgments very complicated. On the last day of class the professor said to us, "I suppose you all feel a little insecure about how to respond to the things people may confess about their business practices."

His next words were, "Don't worry. *It will never come up in Confession.*"

He was right.

FACING THE COMMITMENT OF STEWARDSHIP

In the ritual of Baptism, the words of anointing are, "As Christ was anointed Priest, Prophet, and King, so live always as a member of his body." These words give us our job description as Christians. But more than likely, they were never explained to any of us, and we never asked what they committed us to do.

That is one reason why we just don't think to confess sins against social justice. We haven't really accepted, as a basic moral obligation inherent in our Baptism, the serious duty to work for the reform and renewal of society. We see that as the special call or preoccupation of "social activists," not as an essential element of our anointed stewardship.

In his response to the Synod on Reconciliation, John Paul II pointed out that the social structures, policies, and behavior we blame in a general way on the "system" or the "culture" are really

the result of the accumulation and concentration of many personal sins...of those who cause or support evil or who exploit it; of those who are *in a position to avoid, eliminate or at least limit certain social evils* but who *fail to do so out of laziness, fear* or the conspiracy of silence, through secret complicity or indifference; of those who *take refuge in the supposed impossibility of changing the world* and also of those who *sidestep the effort and sacrifice required*, producing specious reasons of higher order. The real responsibility, then, lies with individuals.

His reason for writing is to

appeal to the consciences of all, so that each may *shoulder his or her responsibility* seriously and courageously *in order to change* those disastrous conditions and intolerable situations.[1]

This is a summons to accept our identity as *stewards*.

To be anointed a "steward of the kingship of Christ" is to

be consecrated and committed to *take responsibility* for establishing the "reign of God" over every area and activity of human life on earth. That is a serious, constant, daily task. What it commits us to is the exercise of *leadership* to bring about *change*.

Leadership and authority are not synonymous. The function of authorities is to hold the community together. The function of leaders is to move it forward. Leaders do not have to have authority, and authorities may be very limited in their gifts of leadership. Very few people are invested with authority, but all Christians are called to exercise leadership according to their circumstances and abilities. Anyone who sees what needs to be done in a given situation is expected to exercise leadership by taking initiative. This consists in taking appropriate action: whether by doing oneself what is required, or by calling it to the attention of those who have the ability or the authority to get it done. The primary sin against leadership is silence.

A cover-up for the sin of silence is negative criticism and gossip. When we gripe and complain to others who can do nothing about the evil we see, we are simply hiding our own cowardice or laziness under cheap words. We are firing blanks into the air because we want to look involved, but we are afraid to join the fight. This should be brought to Confession.

GETTING DOWN TO PRACTICE

What is required of us as stewards is first to *notice* what needs to be changed around us and then to *try* to do something about it.

We will not notice all we should unless we have taken conscious responsibility for everything around us. As stewards of the kingship of Christ, we need to be alert to anything and everything in our environment that is not consistent with the will and purposes of God — at home, in school, at work, in church, when we party, and when we are alone. We are God's "managers" — without authority to command others or to interfere in their private lives, but with authority from God himself to do anything we legitimately can do to change whatever needs to be changed in our common environment. Every right is based on an obligation. Our right to intervene in what is happening around us is based on our obligation to work to establish the reign of God on earth.

The second thing required is that we *try*. God does not demand success — just fidelity. We need to do what we can and urge others to do what they can, whether it is something as small as picking up a piece of paper on the floor or as great as starting a new political party.

We obviously cannot do everything, or even get partially involved in everything that needs to be done. To be a "faithful steward" we only need to notice what is going on around us, to acknowledge our responsibility, and then make prudent judgments about how to employ our energies. When we report in Confession what we see and how we have decided to respond to it, this can be a source of clarification and encouragement.

THE SIN OF SILENCE

Most often neglected is the duty to speak up to authorities. As "stewards of the kingship of Christ" we have an explicit obligation — and therefore an implicit right — to do this. This includes, with special necessity in our day, the obligation the laity have to call the clergy, including bishops, to account. Paul opposed Peter "to his face" when Peter was too cowardly to stand up against the "Pharisee party" in the Church (Galatians 2:11–14). In today's Pharisee party the same legalistic, carping mentality is putting up all sorts of stumbling blocks against effective pastoral ministry, and too often Church authorities or ministers are reluctant or afraid to oppose it.

The members of the "law and order" party speak up — predictably in negative opposition to what is progressive, pastoral, or prophetic. But almost no one speaks up against the legalism, clericalism, or "triumphalism" (the pompous projection of ecclesial power and prestige) that were identified and rejected by the bishops in the first session of the Second Vatican Council. An arrogant pastor will not be reported to his bishop or reprimanded. Nor will the rigid legalists who "tie up heavy burdens, hard to bear, and lay them on the shoulders of others; while they themselves are unwilling to lift a finger to move them" (Matthew 23:4). To preach conservative heresy — making the rules stricter than they are, distorting doctrines through ignorance or narrowness, denying the Eucharist to those who have a right to receive it — is pretty safe. No one will complain to the bishop. But anyone who leans to the left is in danger of instant denunciation. There is a saying in the Vatican, "The right writes." The left fumes in silence. That is a sin against stewardship.

Christians rarely accuse themselves in Confession of not confronting their pastors. But if they know their pastors are wrong, this makes them (objectively) guilty of unconfessed sin against their baptismal responsibility as stewards. Ignorance may excuse one from subjective guilt, but does not exempt one from objective consequences. Unfaithful stewardship allows the reign of God to stagnate. The failure of Catholics to bring this to Confession allows their infidelity and that of others to remain undiagnosed and deadly.

All of us are equally responsible for the fidelity, the growth, and the mission of the People of God. And as the People of God we are all responsible for bringing his reign to the world:

> An eternal and universal kingdom:
>
> a kingdom of truth and life,
>
> a kingdom of holiness and grace,
>
> a kingdom of justice, love and peace.[2]

This requires us to be attentive to what is happening around us, and to be outspoken about what we see and how we think things could be improved.

We need to do this with humility and love. St. Paul gives guidelines for effectively building up the Church and the world. Stewards who make suggestions in love are "patient, kind, not envious or boastful or arrogant or rude." They do not "insist on their own way; are not irritable or resentful." They do not gloat over others' mistakes or push factional preferences, but "rejoice in the truth." Faithful stewards "bear all things" with serenity, "believe all things" until facts convince them otherwise, "hope all things" of others, relying on their goodness and grace, and "endure all things" that must be endured to bring about the ultimate reign of God. They are aware that they "know only in part and prophesy only in part," that they don't have all the answers. But they are willing to do what they can, tentative and incomplete though it may be, confident that "when the complete comes, the partial will come to an end." Then all of the redeemed will be perfectly "one in faith and in the knowledge of God's Son, and *form that perfect man* who is *Christ come to full stature*" (1 Corinthinans 13:4–10; Ephesians 4:11–13).

This is the hope that stewardship is built on. Confession is the sacrament of accountability that keeps us active and alert as stewards of the kingship of Christ.

THE MYSTICISM OF ACCOUNTABILITY

Awareness of accountability as "stewards of the manifold grace of God" is awareness of having a gift to be accountable for. It is the experience of one's existence as entrusted relationship, of one's life as a sharing in the meaning and purpose of Christ's life, of one's time as having eternal value. This awareness is a mystical experience. We need to acknowledge and embrace it in Confession.

CHAPTER SIX

A Bird's-Eye Review

Let's look at the acts involved in Confession

A HUMBLE BUT ENCOURAGED HEART

*C*ontrition is the logical starting point of
Confession. But we need to see contrition in a
more generic way, not just as sorrow for some particular sin (although this might spark the process
on a given occasion), but as the abiding sense we all have that
we stand imperfect before God, always in need of his mercy
and forgiveness.

All contrition should be grounded in a fundamental sense of
human weakness. We do not start with the assumption, "I am
perfect except for...." That is Phariseeism: the identification of
religion with observance of the law, combined with a sense of

righteousness if we are not conscious of any laws we might be breaking. Rather, we stand before the infinite holiness of God, all presumption annihilated in his presence. We are deeply conscious that we do not know him enough to praise him adequately, appreciate him enough to love him as we should, or reverence him enough to serve him as we ought. Our prayer is the cry of the psalmist:

> Have mercy on me, O God, according to your steadfast love; according to your abundant mercy blot out my transgressions....For I know my transgressions, and my sin is ever before me....
>
> You desire truth in one's inward being; therefore teach me wisdom in my secret heart....Let me hear joy and gladness.... Hide your face from my sins, and blot out all my iniquities.
>
> Create in me a clean heart, O God, and put a new and right spirit within me. Do not cast me away from your presence, and do not take your holy spirit from me. Restore to me the joy of your salvation, and sustain in me a willing spirit.... A broken and contrite heart, O God, you will not despise. (Psalm 51)

In addition to this, we all feel we must admit with St. Paul, who even though he knew he had become a "new creation" by grace — "It is no longer I who live, but it is Christ who lives in me" — nevertheless felt compelled to add:

> I am of the flesh, sold into slavery under sin. I do not understand my own actions.... For I do not do the good I want, but the evil I do not want is what I do....I delight in the law of God in my inmost self, but I see in my members another law at war with the law of my mind, making me captive to the law of sin that dwells in my members. Wretched man that I

am! Who will rescue me from this body of death? (Galatians
2:20; Romans 7:14-24)

The answer is Paul's own answer: "Thanks be to God
through Jesus Christ our Lord!" We are not simply slaves to
the "flesh" — in bondage to the cultural conditioning we are
exposed to through physical interaction with others. Paul says,
"You are not in the flesh; you are in the Spirit, since the Spirit
of God dwells in you."

The first effect of contrition is awareness of he Holy Spirit
dwelling in us.

We experience the Holy Spirit — and we need to own that
it is a mystical experience, an awareness of the life of grace —
when we find that something within us is able, through the
enlightenment of faith, to look down on something else in us.
The confession of sin is the profession and experience of our
faith, of the conformity of our heart and mind with God's heart
and mind, even though we are failing in our external behavior.
St. Augustine says it:

> Whoever confesses sins....is already working with God. God
> indicts your sins. If you also indict them, you are joined with
> God....When you begin to abhor what you have done, it is
> then that your good works are beginning, since you are ac-
> cusing yourself of your evil works. The beginning of good
> works is the confession of evil works. You do the truth and
> come to the light.[1]

As we said before, it is our ideals that we reveal in
Confession far more than our sins. This is a revelation of the
life of grace within us. This tells us who we are. We experience ourselves as "being Christ" by Baptism, having died and

risen in him: This is "the Spirit of him who raised Jesus from the dead," giving "life to our mortal bodies also through his Spirit that dwells in us...." We experience ourselves as sons and daughters of the Father "in Christ" the Son:

> For all who are led by the Spirit of God are children of God.
> For you did not receive a spirit of slavery to fall back into
> fear, but you have received a spirit of adoption. When we
> cry, "Abba! Father!" it is that very Spirit bearing witness with
> our spirit that we are children of God. (Romans 8:11–16)

The point is that *contrition* is a mystical experience. To acknowledge how bad we are is to discover how good we are! That is why the call to repentance is always a joyful call: God does not just invite us to turn away from sin and return to a reasonable, human way of acting. When God calls to repentance, he always adds the promise of the rich gift of the Holy Spirit raising us to a new level of life, letting us think with the thoughts of God himself and love as God loves. "I will put my law *within* them, and I will *write it on their hearts*; and I will be their God, and they shall be my people" (Jeremiah 31: 31–34). In Confession *we should seek and claim the mystical experience of graced identity, union with Jesus in mind and heart*, by recognizing our sins as sin and our contrition as faith.

"Gnothi seauton": Know yourself

The *examination of conscience* should be another mystical experience — specifically, one of *enlightenment*. But for this to be what it should be, we have to obey Jesus' words to Peter and "put out into the deep" (Luke 5:4). A shallow survey of com-

mandments kept and broken is an experience of God that is
as minimal as the level of religious observance under review.
To experience the Holy Spirit we have to go to the words the
Spirit inspired in Scripture, measuring our lives against the
words of Jesus and the example of his life on earth. We are
called to be *disciples*. Our behavior should reflect serious study
of the mind and heart of Christ.

We should also go deeper into self-knowledge. What we
need to bring to light in Confession is not just our sins but
their causes. If I repeatedly confess "being impatient," I should
dig for the root of this. Do I expect too much of myself, of others, or of God's timeline for the world? Do I need to shift some
of my burden onto God's shoulders and stop thinking everything depends on me? I may find that my real sin is not impatience at all but lack of trust in God.

When John the Baptizer called to repentance, he said, "The
ax is laid to the root of the tree." If we don't get to the roots of
our sins, we will just keep confessing the same old things un-
productively forever. If my recurring sin is acting out of anger,
I need to ask, not just what I am angry about, but why it upsets
me so much. My real problem may be a chronic anger about
something quite different from the particular incidents that
trigger it. That is the anger I need to address. And if my anger
is disproportionate to the cause, by discovering what is ampli-
fying it I may come to see something that is diminishing my
life in more ways than I was aware of.

A good way to discover the causes of sin in my life is to look
for the results of grace in my life. What is blocking them? Am I
experiencing the "fruit of the Spirit" (Galatians 5:22–23)? Is my
life normally characterized by love, joy, peace? If not, why not?
Where the fruit is missing, something is wrong with the tree.

Jesus himself said mediocre fruit calls for pruning (John 15:2).

The examination of conscience is not just an exercise in psychological self-knowledge, much less navel-gazing. It is something we engage in after prayer and through prayer, and is itself a prayer form. It is essentially reflection on God's word and discernment of the action of the Holy Spirit in our hearts. It is an effort to understand what is going on between ourselves and God.

We can grow into more effective discernment of God's movements in our hearts through daily use of the *Awareness Exercise* taught and insisted upon by St. Ignatius of Loyola for all who take the spiritual life seriously. Take five minutes at noon (walking down the hall for lunch) and in the evening (when you take your shower?) to ask yourself, "Did my mood change today?" If so, ask when and why. See if God is "telling you something" through that.[2]

The Awareness Exercise:

- To begin, *clear your mind*, focus on the fact God is present to you, where you are, and ask God's help.
- First step: *Get in touch with your feelings.* Look for any change of mood you experienced during the time you are reviewing. Did you start feeling good or bad, better or worse, after some thought or choice you made? When, where, why did this happen?
- Next, *make a judgment* about the source of these feelings. Is God perhaps giving or taking away your peace to help keep you on course? Is there something you need to reconsider, to look at more deeply? Take a stance toward the decisions

and choices of the day. Decide if they were right, wrong, or doubtful. See if you feel at peace with your stance.

- Then *look to the future*. Take a deliberate stance of faith, encouragement, love. Decide how you want to respond to the feeling. Determine your course of action. Speak to God about what you are going to do now. Ask his help.

Taken seriously, the examination of conscience is an exercise of the examined life in which *we seek and claim the mystical experience of enlightenment through discipleship.*

ENFLESHED ENCOUNTER

The *confession of sins* is the essence of Confession, but we misunderstand it unless we realize that what it is, essentially, is a mystical encounter with Jesus Christ.

One Sunday afternoon in the 1930s in the parish in Germany where he was pastor, Fr. Bernard Häring was conducting the weekly religious instruction. This particular Sunday he was talking about Confession, and began by asking the congregation: "What is the most important thing about Confession?" A woman in the front pew immediately answered: "Telling your sins to the priest. That's why we call it *confession.*" Fr. Häring said, "Confessing your sins is important, but it's not the most important thing."

A man towards the back called out: "Contrition! Being sorry for your sins! The whole thing doesn't work without contrition." Fr. Häring said, "That's right, it doesn't 'work' without contrition; but I don't think that contrition is the *most* important thing."

A man over on the left side of church spoke up: "It's the

examination of conscience. Unless you examine your conscience, you don't know what you have to be sorry for and you don't know what to confess. Anybody can see that the examination of conscience is the most important thing." Fr. Häring wasn't satisfied with this answer either.

A young woman on the aisle tried: "It's the penance — giving back the things you stole. Unless you do the penance, it doesn't count." The congregation could tell by Fr. Häring's face that he still hadn't heard the most important thing. An uneasy silence fell over the church as people tried to think.

In the silence a little girl in the third pew said: "Father, I know what's most important. It's what Jesus does!" Fr. Haring smiled. She had it right.[3]

We go into the confessional to talk to Jesus. Talking through the confessor is just what makes the interaction human, or *sacramental*. Remember that a sacrament is an invisible interaction with God embodied in a visible interaction with human beings. In Confession we speak to Jesus with human words, and we hear him speaking back with a human voice. Admittedly, the confessor is not always an apt instrument to transmit the tone and content of the counsel Jesus wishes to give. But Jesus' acceptance, love, and forgiveness are always transmitted.

This encounter with Jesus acting through the priesthood of the confessor (whether an ordained minister or not) makes us conscious of our own priesthood. In Baptism we were anointed to share in the consecration and mission of Jesus as "*Priest, Prophet, and King*." When we experience Jesus ministering to us in others, it moves us to "go and do likewise": to "have mercy" on others (Luke 10:37); to forgive as we have been forgiven (Matthew 18:32–34); to heal and give life as Jesus did in extension of the Father's love (John 5:14-22). We who have met Jesus in the flesh must let others meet him enfleshed in us.

With the experience of God, as with other things, "what goes around comes around." What we receive through Christ's self-expression in others we give by letting Christ express himself in us. We give what we receive, and in giving we receive more.

That is why, in every Confession, *we seek and we should claim the mystical experience of encounter with Jesus in the flesh.*

"FRUIT WORTHY OF REPENTANCE"

Doing the "penance" assigned in sacramental reconciliation was originally a way to repair the damage one's defection did to the community's morale. Every sin is an implicit denial of faith, or at least calls into question one's commitment to the faith that binds Christians together in experienced "fellowship of the Holy Spirit." The early Church required apostates to do long and rigorous public penance to reestablish the credibility of their Christian profession.

We do not have to deny the faith formally to appear to be deserters. The bishops shouldered the blame for all of us in the Second Vatican Council by admitting that "to the extent that we...fail in our religious, moral, or social life, we must be said to conceal rather than to reveal the true nature of God and of religion."[4] To act in a way contrary to faith is to conceal — and effectively deny — the reality of one's faith. This bears counter-witness to Jesus. It gives "aid and comfort to the enemy."

To make up for this — and repair the damage we have done — we must do more than just return to the "straight and narrow." We must bear a positive witness to the Gospel that is more striking and powerful that the negative witness we have borne by our sins and mediocrity — a witness that "evokes admiration and conversion," that "becomes the preaching and proclamation of the Good News." We need to live in a way that raises eyebrows, to adopt a lifestyle that stirs up "irresistible questions" in the hearts of those who see how we live. Only in this way can we make up for the damage we have done to Christ's image in the world.

> The Gospel must be proclaimed by witness....[by Christians who] radiate...faith in values that go beyond current values, and...hope in something...one would not dare to imagine. Through this wordless witness these Christians stir up irresistible questions in the hearts of those who see how they live: Why are they like this? Why do they live in this way? What or who is it that inspires them?

Paul VI maintains this is the only way to show that our faith in Jesus Christ is authentic:

> Here lies the test of truth, the touchstone of evangelization: it is unthinkable that people should accept the Word and give themselves to the Kingdom without becoming persons who bear witness to it and proclaim it in their turn.[5]

To take on the mission of bearing witness to Jesus Christ by a *way of life* that "stirs up irresistible questions in the hearts of those who see how we live" is every bit as demanding as doing penance by standing at the door of the church in sackcloth and ashes for a determinate number of years. This is "penance" for a lifetime. And it involves everything in our lifestyle.

This "penance" is incumbent on us all:

All Christians by the example of their lives and the witness of the word, wherever they live, have an obligation to
manifest the "new self" which they put on in Baptism and
to reveal the power of the Holy Spirit by whom they were
strengthened at Confirmation, so that others, seeing their
good works, might glorify the Father and more perfectly
perceive the true meaning of human life and the universal
solidarity of humankind.[6]

We embrace as a mystical experience what the Vatican
Council proclaims as a fundamental Christian obligation.
When we *bear witness* by making grace-inspired *changes* in
our lifestyle, we recognize this as the experience of empower-
ment by the Holy Spirit.

By doing penance after Confession *we seek and claim the
mystical experience of the gift and power of the Holy Spirit* en-
abling us to "seek the things that are above" by living and acting as the body of the risen Jesus on earth (Colossians 3:1).

THE "FIRM PURPOSE OF AMENDMENT"

Jesus began his preaching by announcing, "The reign of God is
at hand." It is fitting we should end this inquiry into the sacrament of the examined life by asking what we are doing to bring
it about.

The experience of the Christian life is a five-fold experience of being *transformed, enlightened, empowered, united,*
and *entrusted.* Through Baptism we received a *new identity* as
the body of Christ on earth. We "became Christ." We received
the *light of faith* to be the light of the world as disciples. We

received the *gift of the Spirit* empowering us to bear witness as prophets. We were united with Jesus as "priests in the Priest" so that he could heal and give life to others by *expressing himself* in and through our human words and actions. And as stewards of Christ's kingship we were entrusted with the "manifold grace of God" to *establish the reign of God* on earth.

As stewards of the Kingdom we have a "firm purpose" of *amending the world* by establishing God's reign in our own hearts and in our society. This is the purpose that drives our lives. And we are "firm" in it. The key to stewardship is *fidelity*. Fidelity requires perseverance. The life of the faithful steward is characterized by *waiting* — in faith and fidelity — for Christ to come again. This waiting is sustained by *hope.*

To persevere in *faith* is to persevere in *believing*, in spite of all appearances and experiences to the contrary, that Jesus has won the victory, that he is triumphing over sin and death, that he will "come again in glory to judge the living and the dead, and his Kingdom will have no end." This is the faith that gives hope.

To persevere in *fidelity* is to persevere in *working* to bring about Christ's victory here and now — to establish his Kingdom in our time and space. Fidelity is faith embodied in action. By faith we affirm what will be. By hope we attempt what can be — even when it seems obvious it can't. Faith keeps us awake; hope keeps us active.

> Stay *awake* therefore. You cannot know the day your Lord is coming....
>
> Who is the faithful, farsighted servant whom the master has put in charge of his household...? Happy that servant whom his master finds at work on his return! (Matthew 24:42–46)

To sustain hope when we use Confession, it is important to keep in mind that our *"firm purpose of amendment"* can be generic. And we need to be very clear that it is a promise, not a prediction. We promise to keep trying, whether or not we predict we will succeed. Promises are based on hope, predictions on optimism.

Optimism and hope are two different things. A soldier questioned about the Bataan Death March in World War II said, "The optimists — the ones who said, 'We'll be home before Christmas' — were the first to die." Those who believe that Christ will return in their lifetime — or that they will overcome some particular sin in their life before they are too old to commit it anyway — are optimists. Optimism can bring about the death of faith through disappointment. But "hope does not disappoint us, because God's love has been poured into our hearts through the Holy Spirit that has been given to us" (Romans 5:5). Our hope is based simply on God's love, not on our ability to reform society or even our own lives. Our "firm purpose of amendment" is essentially hope in God and willingness to keep doing whatever we can do, futile or insufficient as it may seem, placing confidence in his eventual victory.

I personally believe that a false understanding of the "firm purpose of amendment" is one of the top reasons why people give up on religion and on the Church.

Try this scenario. You are caught up in some action you have been taught is "mortal sin."[7] You know you are going to keep doing it. Whether you "can't stop" or just don't have sufficient desire to stop is irrelevant; in practice they come down to the same thing.

You see no point in confessing what you are doing, because you don't have a "firm purpose of amendment." You feel it would be hypocritical to say you are "truly sorry." And if you tell the confessor you are not going to stop, he might deny you absolution anyway. So what do you do?

You will probably stop using Confession. You will probably stop receiving Communion. You may eventually stop going to church. You feel alienated and rejected when you are there, so why keep going? Who wants to go to a party where they won't let you sit at the table?

If you are Catholic you may start attending services in another church that either doesn't have Communion or doesn't make an issue of who should receive. Then, at least, you are not giving up on Christianity. But you may just drop out of organized religion altogether. This is disastrous — for you, for your children, if you have any, and for all the people you could help more fully if you were supported and supporting in a community of faith.

What should you do?

This question was raised by a venerated spiritual director in Lyon, France — Père Girardon, SJ — who met with my ordination class in 1961 to prepare us for hearing confessions.

"What do you say to people who tell you a sin in confession and say, 'I'm not going to stop doing it'?"

The Americans in the class answered immediately, "You say you can't give absolution. You need to have a 'firm purpose of amendment' or your sin is not forgiven."

Père Girardon's answer was, "No. You tell them three things."

• *First: don't rationalize.* If it is wrong, don't say it is right. If there is something good and something bad in what you are doing, admit both the good and the bad. Truth is the only safe foundation for anything. Rationalization can lead us into a swamp of false questions and answers that suck us down and down.

Once people think they cannot — or do not want to — live by some particular value taught by Jesus (or required by the rules of the Church), they don't see much point in continuing as a "cafeteria Christian," making up their own menu of morality. They just give up — quite often justifying themselves by looking for, and finding, all sorts of stones they can throw through the Church's own glass windows. They accuse the Church, their parents, and Christians in general of "hypocrisy" because of all the values churchgoers are not living up to — and these are not hard to find, if anyone wants to look! Then, having decided that others are worse than they are, they feel justified in saying that if they themselves cannot live by one of those values, they can at least stop associating with the churchgoers as if they were hypocrites also. That is why rationalization is deadly.

- *Second: admit your weakness.* Humility is truth, and the truth of human beings is that we grow into perfection slowly, through many trials and errors, failures, and recommitments. To pretend, even to ourselves, that we will not fail and fail badly is to lose contact with our own reality. And that breaks our contact with everything else. So we admit our weakness and we live with it. If God can, why shouldn't we?

Admitting weakness is not something we were brought up to do. Even if we never heard the word "Pelagianism," we grew up assuming that only two things were required to avoid sin: grace and free will. And since grace could be taken for granted, it was all up to our free will. To say we were "weak" was a cop-out. So if we sinned we were simply choosing not to do what God desired. Period. No excuses and no mercy.

I sometimes tell people that overcoming impossible obstacles in the spiritual life is like sailing through the locks on the Panama Canal. When you arrive at a lock, you can't push your way through by brute force. The obstacle in front of you is the land mass itself. So the only solution is, first, to cut off all retreat. In a lock they lower a barrier behind you. Next they let the water flow into the lock until the ship rises to the level of the canal beyond the lock. Then the ship just sails over the barrier.

When you acknowledge your weakness, you don't just go limp and whine. You start a "spiritual fitness program." You acknowledge you haven't been thinking about God enough, praising him enough, appreciating him enough, reflecting on his words enough, using prayer and sacraments enough.

When you face a temptation you are not able to conquer, you are like the king Jesus spoke about, who, "going out to wage war against another king, sits down first and considers whether he is able with ten thousand to oppose the one who comes against him with twenty thousand" (Luke 14:31). If not, Jesus says he had better admit his weakness. But he still has two choices: come to terms with the enemy or gather more troops.

In the spiritual life, coming to terms with sin is not an option. We start building up our strength. When we have grown enough in grace, we just sail over the temptation that used to be insurmountable. The "firm purpose of amendment" doesn't have to focus on the sin we "can't stop." It can focus instead on using the means that will eventually make us able to stop. This brings us to Père Girardon's third suggestion:

- *Third: keep going to Confession and Communion.*

Here the Americans, more steeped in legalism than the French, erupted in protest: "That's hypocrisy! How can you say you are sorry for what you have done if you are going to keep doing it? That is what we are always being accused of: 'You Catholics commit sins all week, go to Confession on Saturday, receive Communion on Sunday, and then go out and do the same thing all over again.' It's hypocrisy."

Père Girardon gave his answer in one line. I remember it word for word: "*Dieu ne demande pas l'impossible, mon père.*" God doesn't ask the impossible. He sees our weakness and our struggles. He looks at our heart more than at our behavior. If he sees that we want to love him, want to believe in him, and want to follow his way — but are just unable right now to do it — he has patience with us. He encourages us to do whatever we can, and to keep trying.

What would Jesus say to someone who can't stop sinning? I do not know. But I know what he would not say. He would not say, "Well, since you don't have a firm purpose of amendment, there is nothing I can do for you. Go away, and when you are able to save yourself from this sin, come back and we'll celebrate your reconciliation."

The Savior doesn't send people away to save themselves. And neither should the confessor who represents him in Confession. Jesus doesn't cut us off from forgiveness or Communion. It was from the Father's example that Jesus took what he told Peter:

"Lord, when my brother or sister wrongs me, how often must I forgive? Seven times?"

"No," Jesus replied, "not seven times. I say, seventy times seven times" (Matthew 18:21).

And that's on a daily basis!

"If the same person sins against you seven times a day, and turns back to you seven times and says, 'I repent,' you must forgive" (Luke 17:4).

That is what Jesus does. If we are more demanding than he is, of ourselves or of others, we are unfaithful servants.

It is not hypocrisy to be sorry and not sorry at the same time — sorry for what is wrong in what you are doing but not completely sorry for all of it. Or sorry for what you are doing but not sorry enough to stop. This is a description of weakness, not malice. You may not be fully repentant, but you are not fully committed to evil either. There can be a question about "full consent" on both sides.

When we come to Confession, we have a sufficiently "firm purpose of amendment" if we say to God sincerely, here and now — and generically — "I will try to go as long as I can without sinning." We don't have to spell it out. And we don't have to look ahead.

We might be confused about what "sinning" really means in our case. We might not know what "as long as I can" means, either. We may feel confident it means forever, or we may feel sure we won't last five minutes. And we might be wrong in both cases!

The crucial question is, "Do I have the deliberate intention, right now, of committing this sin at a particular time, in a particular place that I have already decided on?" If not, if it is just that I don't think I can refrain from doing it again or for very long (and may even feel pretty sure about when that will be), then I am in actual fact able to say, no matter how weakly, "Lord, I will try to go as long as I can without sinning." That is enough for God.

When we make a promise like this, we should be very conscious that there is a hidden card in the deck: God's. For all we know, God might zap us with a grace so strong we will never sin again. Or we might drop dead of a heart attack in the next instant, in which case we will have kept our commitment until death! The important thing is we aren't able to predict what we are going to do in the future, even the immediate future; what we are able to do is desire sincerely to respond to God right now as best we can and to promise that — in general terms.

All Jesus asks is good will. He just asks us to do our best, meaning the best we are able to do right now. It was Jesus who said, "Do not worry about tomorrow, for tomorrow will bring worries of its own. Today's trouble is enough for today" (Matthew 6:34). We do what we can do in the present and entrust the future to God. We live in the "now" of reality, remaining open to growth and change.

A promise is not a prediction. And a commitment to keep trying is not a guarantee of instant reformation. If we have the realism not to rationalize, the humility to admit our weakness, and a deep desire to love and serve God with undivided hearts, what more does God ask of us except that we should do the best we actually can do at the moment and trust in him for the rest?

The sign of our good will, and our lifeline to the Church, is continuing Confession and Communion — or even Communion without Confession until we can find a confessor who will understand us and help us to "hang in there."[8]

A good confessor will know how to coach us through the crisis, how to keep us from deviating too far off course or going off the deep end. Confession — with the right confessor — can also stop us from getting so discouraged about ourselves that we just give up. Jesus said, "Those who are well have no need of a physician, but those who are sick" (Matthew 9:12). In the same spirit we could say that those who are successfully dealing with sin in their lives are not the ones who have most need of a confessor. It is those who are faced with sins they cannot cope with who should cling to the ongoing help of Confession as to a life raft.

The "firm purpose of amendment" should be a mystical experience! It is not just a human judgment about what we can or are willing to do. It is an act of trust, based on divine faith, in what God can and wants to do.

It is commonplace to call for this kind of trust when we weigh our prospects for establishing the reign of God on earth. Faithful stewardship means we keep trying to reform society, even when, in our human judgment, we are helpless and hopeless. We need to exercise the same trust when we feel helpless to turn away from sins in our own life and when the very prospect of getting out of sin seems hopeless.

The "firm purpose of amendment" is an unrestricted, unconditional act of hope in what God can do. No matter how weak and unwilling we find ourselves to be, we keep coming to God and to Confession, "hoping against hope," as Abraham did (Romans 4:18), and believing that "what is impossible for humans is possible for God" (Luke 18:27). We confess our sins as sins, acknowledge our weakness, tell God we are willing to do whatever we are willing to do, and trust that some way, some day, he will "deliver us from evil."

Going into the confessional doesn't mean we are never going to sin again. It means we are never going to stop dealing with Jesus the Savior — and dealing with him through the Church and sacraments — until Christ comes again. In the strength and weakness of our "firm purpose of amendment" *we seek and claim the mystical experience of believing in Christ's victory.*

Sin should never be the focus in a Christian life. Our focus should be on God as revealed in Jesus Christ and revealing himself still in Christ's body on earth and in the action of the Holy Spirit. Confession should never be an obstacle to interaction with God. Confession should be an experience of light and love and life — a mystical experience.

May the God of hope fill you with all joy and peace in believing, so that you may abound in hope by the power of the Holy Spirit. (Romans 15:13)

CHAPTER SEVEN

The Empty Tomb

Life Through Death

Confession is not just something we do. It is a mystery we enter into. It is an experience. In Confession we relive the mystery of our Baptism, through which we entered into the true reality of our redemption: the mystery of dying and rising in Christ who died on the cross and rose again precisely so that we might die and rise "in him."

In this way, and only through the mystery of this, can we understand that our sins are not just "forgiven" but "taken away."

We go into the confessional as into a tomb. It is the tomb of the crucified Christ, in whose body, when he was taken down from the cross, we were included. We go in to see his wounds, to confront and to confess the sins we put into that body.

But it is an empty tomb.

An angel meets us at the entrance. He says to us what he said to the women who went to the tomb to anoint Jesus' body: "Why do you look for the living among the dead? He is not here, but has risen" (Luke 24:5).

"Why do you look for Jesus among the dead works of your past? You will not find him there. The past is wiped away, annihilated in his death. The burying place of your sins is empty. The Lamb of God has conquered sin and death. He has *taken away* the sins of the world. He is not here; he has been raised... He is going *ahead of you* to Galilee; there you will see him."

We go to Confession to experience the mystery of the death and rising of Jesus, the mystery of our death and rising in him. Our sins are not just forgiven; they are "*taken away*." Our past is an empty tomb. Our future is with Jesus who is calling us to follow him into the future — into a new life of mission, a life of "fruitful labor" in union of mind and heart and will with him (Philippians 1:22).

It took the death of a sixteen-year-old girl in Africa for me to realize this. Out of my sin that brought about her death God gave me new life, new understanding of the mystery of redemption. And a new understanding of love.

Her name was Tar-m-al. The whole story is this.

I had driven to a village twenty miles away to see a priest-doctor who had a clinic. A young Italian student went with me. When we were getting back into my pickup truck to return, two young girls from my mission approached to ask for a ride. They said they were from Moyo, a village where I had a mission. It was on the way; I had to pass through it to go home, and I also had to stop there to see the chief about some mission business. So I told them to get into the back of the truck, since there was no room in the cab.

It is important to know that, if I hadn't needed to stop there already, I may not have taken them. This is hard to understand, but the reason was double. First, every time anyone got into a truck in Chad, a swarm of people instantly gathered like flies, wanting a ride to somewhere — sometimes for a serious reason, sometimes for a made-up one. There were frequently more people asking to get in than the springs of the truck could support. What this brought about in me — and I confess it as a sin — was an attitude. Unconsciously, I began to see people as annoyances. In my heart, I felt as if they were a swarm of flies, and my spontaneous reaction was to brush them away.

The second reason was the roads. They were made of laterite, a rocky earth that in the dry season formed ripples. Driving over the road was like driving over a washboard or a corrugated roof. In first gear you literally could not keep the truck from swerving from one side of the road to the other. In second gear everything vibrated so badly that the nuts and bolts began to come loose. It was only when you reached fifty miles per hour that the truck settled down and the ride became normal.

So you didn't like to stop. And I probably would not have given the girls a ride if I weren't going to stop in Moyo anyway. If you judge me harshly for this, you will be right. I judge myself now more harshly than you do. But remember: you haven't been there.

I stopped in Moyo, finished my business, and started off down the road. I had just reached fifty miles an hour and got the truck under control again when there was a banging on the roof. I looked back and was amazed to see that the girls were still in the truck. They were shouting, "Stop here! Sohongo!"

If you can imagine a suburb to a mud-hut village, Sohongo was one. It was the actual name of the village where they lived, just a hundred yards or so past Moyo. I realized the girls had sat in the truck all the time I was conducting my business, just so they could have the thrill of another hundred-yard ride in the truck.

I got mad. That was my sin. I called back through the window: "Sit down! Danamaji."

Danamaji was the name of the village where I lived. It was about five miles further. I was telling them I would stop in Danamaji and they could walk back. Yes, this was a sin. But, to put it in proportion, you have to know that in Chad people would walk ten miles to come to Mass and never even think about it. Still, this was my sin.

The girls banged on the roof again, and I shouted at them again to sit down. The thought vaguely crossed my mind, "They wouldn't jump, would they?" I yelled again, "Sit down!"

Then the student in the cab with me said, "Stop!"

As soon as he said it, I knew what had happened. One of the girls had jumped.

I remember how surprised I was as a child the first time I got off my bicycle before it came to a stop and I fell forward. I learned about "inertia" before I heard the word. These girls had never experienced that. They had no idea what it was like to jump out of a truck going fifty miles an hour. The one who did died almost instantly.

I was brought up, like everyone else in my generation, to see my religion as law-observance. And amid all the horror of Tarm-al's death, I remember the thought going through my mind, "What sin have I committed?" The answer was immediate and obvious: "A venial sin of impatience."

My reaction was just as immediate and obvious. The differ-ence between "mortal" and "venial" sin doesn't matter much when someone is lying dead in the road.

I saw that Tar-m-al was dead or dying, and I called for water. I gave her conditional Baptism. And then, because there were no ambulances in Chad, we put her back in the truck and I drove for the hospital in Fort Archambault as fast as I could. She was pronounced dead on arrival.

On the way I had stopped in Danamaji to pick up Joseph Radjitan, my catechist, to accompany me and translate if nec-essary. When I told him the story, he asked, "Why did you bap-tize her? You baptized her last Easter." I had baptized her with my own hand. She was my "daughter in Christ." And I didn't even remember.

There is more to the story, but it is enough to say that her funeral was the hardest act of ministry I ever performed. It was not nearly as hard on me, of course, as it was on her parents. But are you picking up something here? Are you noticing how much of this story is about me? About what I felt? About the effects on me rather than on others? That is an important part of the story.

I went to see my bishop. My opening words were, "I think I am under a curse." What I meant was that I was not living that bad a life — I wasn't committing any serious sins and was trying to do my job — but still this terrible thing happened. To me.

An American bishop probably would have understood my words as inviting a dialogue. The French bishop (one of the best I have ever met) just looked at me and said, "You are not under a curse."

So I decided to put the event out of my mind. I went to

Confession, got "forgiven," as I understood it then, and didn't feel any better at all. I was glad God was not mad at me, glad God was not going to punish me for my sin, glad he forgave me. But I was still the man who had killed that girl, and all the forgiveness in the world could not change that. When my confessor spoke the words of absolution, "Through the ministry of the Church, may God grant you pardon and peace," I received pardon. But I didn't get peace.

Two years later, when I made my thirty-day retreat, I confronted this. The first words that came to my mind when I began to think about it were an echo of my words to the bishop: "Christ became a curse for us, hanging on the tree." From this God led me to Saint Paul's teaching: "For our sakes God made him who did not know sin to *be sin*, so that in him we might become the very holiness of God" (Galatians 3:13; 2 Corinthians 5:21).

Yes, I was under a curse. The human race is under a curse, a curse of our own making. Millions of years of individual, personal sins have created the environment into which we are born. Every act of sin has put something into the environment that never goes away. We are all born into an infected culture. Before we are old enough to know what we are doing or to be guilty of it, we are "programmed" to distorted attitudes and destructive patterns of behavior. No one escapes.

But our own, personal sins add to this. I realized that I had fallen into an attitude that saw people as annoyances instead of as my brothers and sisters — or in Tar-m-al's case — as my daughter in Christ. When I dealt with people, I wasn't *aware* of the mystery I was dealing with. Or of the mystery of Jesus in me, Jesus wanting to love and act with me, in me, and through me to give life to all I dealt with. I wasn't aware.

I realized this was the fruit of my failure to pray. If anyone had an "excuse" for not spending time in meditation and
prayer, I did. I had twenty-five villages to visit and care for, plus
all the other innumerable tasks that go with living alone in a
village where no one else can even fix a flashlight. One morning, walking over to the church, I stopped "just for a moment"
at the cattle pen to relieve a cow of a huge tick I had been
noticing for three days. I got so involved that, by the time I finished, I realized I had forgotten entirely to celebrate Mass!

I had no less excuse, and no more excuse, for not praying as
I should than anyone else has. I didn't have the time to pray as
I should. I didn't make the time to pray as I should. And I real-
ized the consequences.

I was seeing Tar-m-al as an annoyance instead of as my
daughter in Christ. I became painfully aware that if she had
been my blood daughter when the idea crossed my mind that
she might possibly jump out of the truck, I would have stopped
on a dime. But I wasn't seeing her as my daughter. Because I
was not praying. I was not reflecting on the mystery of who
she was, who I was, and of the relationship between us.

Yes, I was under a curse. The curse was that I was failing to
love.

And then I asked myself: "What does 'Tar-m-al' mean in
the Ngama language?" "Tar" means "love." "M" stands for "me."
"Al" means "not." "Tar-m-al" means "You love me not."

This was really her name. And I knew that God was speaking it to me in every person whom I failed to see with his eyes
and love with his heart. Each and every one bears her name.
Their name is Tar-m-al.

I am self-centered, self-serving, self-absorbed. If you haven't
figured that out already, you are too kind. But God takes me

as I am, and he threw a crumb of consolation into my self-centeredness. I was mourning the death of this sixteen-year-old girl, cut off by my sin at the blossoming of her life. What might she have become? What name might she have made for herself?

And I had this thought. Condemn me for it if you will. But, without diminishing my sin or the tragedy of her death, it is true. Tar-m-al's name might never have been known outside of her African village. It would have been known to her family, to her husband and children, to her friends, and nothing can replace that. But God draws good even out of evil; he makes the best out of that which is nothing. And I have the hope that through my experience, and through my telling of the story, which is always painful to me, the name of Tar-m-al may take its place in the world. I hope it will be spoken; I hope it will resound in the hearts of all who hear her story.

"My name is Tar-m-al. You meet me in everyone you fail to love. Wake up and recognize me. *My name is 'Tar-m-al' — 'You do not love me.'*"

I told this story in a high school retreat. At the end of the retreat I asked the students to write down one thing they were going to do as a result of the retreat. One boy's paper said, "On the mirror where I shave, I am going to write 'Tar-m-al.'"

It is written on the wall of every confessional, in invisible, burning ink. It is the cause of every sin, the one thing we will be judged for.

Saint John of the Cross said, "In the evening of our lives we will be judged by love." In Confession we face that judgment ahead of time. We judge ourselves while we are held in the arms of our Father, held to the heart of our merciful Savior, surrounded and embraced by the Spirit of his love.

Jesus said, "If you love me, you will keep my commandments." And his commandments are all contained in one: "I give you a *new commandment*, that you *love one another*. Just as I have loved you, you also should love one another."

That is the reason, the guide, and the goal of Confession. It is an interchange of love.

What is "Mortal Sin"?

A fter hearing confessions for fifty years, one notices certain things rising to the surface that call for special attention. I have focused above on questions about Christian behavior it never occurs to people to ask. Here I want to address a question people never ask, because they think they already have the answer — one so simplistic it is simply false. And it is my belief that this oversimplification is driving people out of the Church.

We quoted above the bishops in the Second Vatican Council who acknowledged that "the rise of atheism" can be blamed in part on the fact that we have been "careless about our instruction in the faith, or have presented its teaching falsely." As a result we have "concealed rather than revealed the true nature of

God and of religion." It is significant, I think, that although the English title of this document is "The Church in the Modern World," the actual Latin title is *Gaudium et Spes*: "Joy and Hope." To identify errors in our teaching or pastoral practice is a joy, because it gives hope. It is in that spirit that I point out an error that has distorted our understanding of Confession and made it in some cases more destructive than beneficial.

The error is to believe it is easy to know whether or not we have committed a "mortal sin."

Confusion through clarity

Catholic teaching about the requirements for true mortal sin is so clear that it creates the illusion of providing an answer. In reality all it does is point us in a direction that can lead to an answer — but only sometimes, and in theory more than in practice.

For someone to be guilty of "mortal sin," three things are required: "serious matter, sufficient knowledge, and full consent of the will." That is deceptively clear. Until we try to apply the norms to real human acts.

The truth is that, unknown to most Catholics, the Church has never officially identified, with the full weight of her teaching authority, any particular act as being "serious matter." She leaves this to common sense. Unfortunately, common sense got left behind in common teaching.

In the early years of Christianity, before the moral theologians began to ticket every action as "mortal" or "venial" sin, the Church seemed to recognize three things clearly as "serious matter": apostasy, murder, and adultery. Later the list was extended, but more through preaching, popular persuasion, and assumptions embodied in pastoral practice than through pronouncements that could claim to be dogma. Even things not important in themselves were accepted as serious matter if they were declared such by Church law, such as missing Mass on one single Sunday, not abstaining from meat on Fridays, or not fasting for a certain amount of time before receiving Communion.

The problem now is that many people are judged to be, and sometimes judge themselves to be, in "mortal sin" when what they are doing is not indisputably "grave matter" at all. To be the "serious matter" required for mortal sin, an action must be not just "bad," not just "real bad," not just "seriously wrong," not just one that causes serious harm to oneself or others. It has to be *evil*.

Granted, the interpretation of the last paragraph depends on how one understands the words. I am trying to express the truth in what I think is current English, fully aware that the same words may carry different weights for different people. For example, I think it is "bad" to smoke — "real bad." It is medically established that it causes "serious harm" to oneself and others. But I wouldn't say automatically it is "seriously wrong" for someone to smoke, just seriously stupid. And I wouldn't call it "evil" or say that smoking is a "mortal sin."

I don't want to offer a whole set of examples, because my point here is that I do not believe it is easy to say whether many things are "serious matter" or not. I would be a fool to try.

If we extend our consideration to the other two requirements for mortal sin, the number of people we can judge without rashness to be guilty of it decreases exponentially.

We were taught in elementary school that we had "sufficient

knowledge" if we could say in English, "This is a mortal sin." And we were giving "full consent" if we did something it was physically in our power not to do. Being out of one's mind in anger and rage might lessen full consent, but cold fear of torture, public disgrace, or other consequences didn't. This was philosophically and psychologically naïve.[1] But the norms we learned in the fifth grade are still commonly applied in pastoral judgments about whether someone is in "mortal sin." The main effect of those pastoral judgments is to exclude people from Communion.

And this has falsified our understanding of Eucharist.

THE "PASS-FAIL" TEST OF EUCHARIST

Being allowed to receive Communion has become a badge of "good standing" in the Church. If the pastor gives you Communion, that says he is officially accepting you as not being guilty — at this moment, at least — of anything the Church calls mortal sin.

The immediate effect of this is to make the pastor hesitate to give Communion to anyone who even *might* be doing something that is objectively mortal sin, even if it is pretty clear that, subjectively, at least, the person is not guilty. The pastor is afraid to cause "scandal" by appearing to accept conduct the Church calls unacceptable.

Archbishop Michael Sheehan of Santa Fe gives clarity of focus: "The primary responsibility for someone receiving Communion is the person himself or herself and their conscience, to come forward to receive. The priest shouldn't be like a watchdog, looking around and finding out who's unworthy."[2]

When people are interiorly moved by grace in their hearts to participate fully in Eucharist, but are told by Church policy that they are in mortal sin and excluded from Communion, they have a predictable reaction. They feel rejected by the Church, angry, and discouraged. If they continue coming to Mass but don't receive Communion, they feel alienated. Most will just stop coming. Many will join other churches where they feel understood and accepted.

I suspect this is a major reason why the second-largest Christian group in the United States, after Catholics, is made up of Catholics who no longer go to Mass. Would you go to a party where they won't let you sit at the table?

Where did we ever get the idea that Communion should be used to separate the sheep from the goats? When and where did we determine that only those who meet a current set of popular benchmarks for "good standing" in the Church have the right to receive Communion? Or worse, that Eucharistic ministers are responsible for judging the state of soul of those who approach for Communion? In authentic Catholic theology, the rock-bottom requirements for Communion are just Baptism and being gifted with God's divine life by grace (not being in "mortal sin"). Canon Law adds some restrictions. For example, Latin-rite Catholics are required to go through an initiation in Christian doctrine before their "First Communion," while Catholics in the Eastern rites are given Communion as infants, as soon as they are baptized. I have no objection to the Latin custom, but in authentic obedience to the mind of the Church I would never let it stop me from giving Communion to small children who are cancer patients at St. Jude Children's Research Hospital in Memphis, where I live. No priest would.

Basically, Church law only bans from Communion those

who "obstinately persist in manifest grave sin."[3] Since what is "grave sin" (or whether someone is "obstinately persisting" in it) is not always "manifest," we should recognize that the law allows room for pastoral judgment. John Paul II himself espoused the time-honored principle: "In what is doubtful, freedom; in what is necessary, unity; in all things, charity."[4] We should lean toward leniency. What should be most "manifest" to our minds is the "first and greatest commandment" of pastoral ministry, which Jesus gave to Peter: "If you love me, *feed my sheep*" (John 21:17).

If exclusion from Eucharist were based on a credible judgment that those excluded were in a real and abiding state of true "mortal sin," the exclusion would make sense. But for this condition to be "manifest" we would have to believe that those excluded are positively "evil" persons. And they themselves would have to know in their hearts that they had consciously and deliberately turned away from God by doing something so evil in itself that God can no longer abide in them or they in him (John 6:56; 15:4).

Since it is so difficult in the concrete to judge what is and is not "mortal sin," and who is and is not subjectively guilty of it, we should choose pastorally not to make that judgment except in extreme and obvious cases. Then Eucharist would be recognized again as what it really is: not just the "bread of angels," but on this earth the strengthening food and sacrament of sinners.

One of the saints mentioned in the canon of the Mass, St. Cyprian (martyred 258 AD), was caught up in the controversy over granting indulgences to shorten the harsh penances required of lapsed Christians who had denied the faith under persecution. Cyprian argued that since the Eucharist was "designed to be a defense and security for those who partake of it," it follows that "we should fortify with the armor of our Lord's banquet those whose safety we are concerned about. How shall they be able to shed their blood for Christ if we deny them the blood of Christ? How shall we fit them to drink the cup of martyrdom, if we will not first admit them to the cup of the Lord?"[5] Should we not say the same of those who are fighting temptation and sin in their lives right now?

There will always be those who are scandalized by others' admission to the table. But we should recognize them as simply echoing "the Pharisees and the scribes [who] were grumbling and saying [about Jesus], 'This fellow welcomes sinners and eats with them'" (Luke 15:2). Is eating with sinners so bad? Does Jesus not do that anymore?

Endnotes

CHAPTER ONE

1. In this book "Church" is capitalized when it refers either to the whole body of Christian believers who recognize themselves as the People of God or (sometimes) to the official Catholic Church. It is not capitalized when it refers to a local church or assembly of believers.

CHAPTER TWO

1. Nevertheless, I will risk a short but doctrinally acceptable explanation of Church teaching. In brief, nothing requires us to believe that God "punishes" or demands any "payment" for sin. "Purgatory" is a misleading term because it suggests that a disembodied soul can exist in time and space after death. It is consistent with Church doctrine to say that our *purification* "after death" (the real meaning of *purgatorium*)

consists in surrendering to the fullness of faith, hope, and love by crying
out "Yes!" to death when it comes. A Christian death requires us to say
willingly, "Father, into your hands I commend my spirit" (Luke 23:46),
instead of mumbling the reluctant "Okay" of mere stoic resignation.
The *Catechism*'s "temporal punishment (*poena*) due to sin" should be
translated as "a transitory *penalty*," or natural consequence, of not doing
during life what we needed to do in order to grow into the fullness
of pure faith, hope, and love (see John of the Cross and the "dark
night of the soul"). The "transitory penalty" is simply the obvious and
inescapable consequence that we must grow into this fullness before
we can be totally united to God in heaven. The level of our faith, hope,
and love at the moment of death makes it easier or harder to make the
transition to a willing, total surrender to God. But the prayers of other
people can help us through that moment. Whether they are offered
before or after the actual time of death is immaterial; they are received
in the time frame of God's all-present "now." In the light of all this,
an authentic understanding of "Purgatory" should inspire us to deep
discipleship, in order to grow into the fullness of faith, hope, and love,
not drive us to superficial devotions garnished with the promise of
"indulgences."

CHAPTER THREE

1. Exhortation after the Synod on "Reconciliation and Penance in the
Mission of the Church," December 2, 1984.

2. "The Church in the Modern World," no. 19. The actual title is
Gaudium et Spes, "Joy and Hope."

3. Pope Paul VI, *Evangelization in the Modern World*, nos. 14, 21, 41.

4. *Ibid*, no. 21. Paul continues: We need to provoke these questions in all who have not been sufficiently evangelized, "whether they are people to whom Christ has never been proclaimed, or baptized people who do not practice, or people who live as nominal Christians but according to principles that are in no way Christian, or people who are seeking, and not without suffering, something or someone whom they sense but cannot name."

5. "Even the pagans recognized the existence of 'divine' moral laws which have 'always' existed and which are written in the depths of the human heart, cf Sophocles (*Antigone*, w. 450-460) and Aristotle (*Rhetoric*, Book I, Chap.15, 1375 a-b)." From John Paul II's exhortation after the Synod on "Reconciliation and Penance in the Mission of the Church," note 183.

6. T*he Splendor of Truth*, nos. 18-21; and "World Day of Peace" address, January 1, 1993.

7. See John 15:13 and *The Gospel of Life*, nos. 22, 25, 34, 39, 40, 47, 51, 52, 53, 55.

8. See Acts 2:38; 8:15–17; 10:45–47; 19:2; 1 Corinthians 2;12; 2 Corinthians 11:4; Galatians 3:2; 6:1.

9. Isaiah actually names only six, but because the Septuagint and Vulgate translations of Isaiah included "piety" instead of listing "fear of the Lord" twice, seven have come down to us.

CHAPTER 4

1. There are exceptions, but this is the norm. In Catholic theology, anyone can baptize, even an atheist. It is just necessary to have the intention of doing whatever the one seeking Baptism is asking, whether the one baptizing believes in it or not. In the other sacraments, the minister must be a baptized member of Christ, but might be a "dead" member. The sins of the minister do not keep Jesus from acting through him or her in the way he promised to act. But to really understand the sacraments we need to look at what is normal, not at what is abnormal and exceptional.

2. Exhortation after the Synod on "Reconciliation and Penance in the Mission of the Church," parag. 29.

3. See Hebrews 8:13 to 10:23. In the New Testament no Christian is called a priest except Jesus himself in the Letter to the Hebrews. However, the First Letter of Peter includes all the baptized in his "holy" and "royal priesthood" (1Peter 2:5–9). Through Baptism we are all "priests in the Priest."

4. John 1:1–18. The words variously translated in Scripture as "grace and truth" or "kindness and fidelity" or simply as "enduring love" are the Hebrew words *hesed* and *emet*, which the *Jerome Biblical Commentary* identifies as the Old Testament's "virtual definition of God."

CHAPTER FIVE

1. Exhortation after the Synod, para. 16.

2. See the Preface for the Mass of Christ the King.

CHAPTER SIX

1. *In Jo. ev.* 12, 13.

2. This method is taught as the "Examen of Conscience" in *The Spiritual Exercises of St. Ignatius*, nos. 24-43 and clarified by George Aschenbrenner, S.J., "Consciousness Examen," in *Review for Religious*, January, 1972. I prefer the title "Awareness Exercise" given to it by the Jesuits at Loyola House in Guelph, Ontario, and have tried to base this explanation of the method on theirs.

3. "Sacrament of Reconciliation: Celebrating the Mercy of God," by Thomas Richstatter, O.F.M., in *Catholic Update*, Saint Anthony Messenger Press, June, 2008.

4. "The Church in the Modern World," no. 19. The actual title of this document is *Gaudium et Spes*, "Joy and Hope."

5. Pope Paul VI, *On Evangelization in the Modern World*, 1975, nos. 15, 21, 24.

6. *Documents of Vatican II*, "Decree on the Church's Missionary Activity," no. 11. See *Ephesians* 4:24.

7. Catechetical teaching about "mortal sin" became so simplistically false in the generations before the Second Vatican Council that it is a prime example of the "careless...instruction in the faith," and "false teaching" by which we "concealed rather revealed the true nature of God and of religion" (see above, page 38). We should not presume lightly that we are in a state of "mortal sin," and never presume this about others.

8. The *Catechism of the Catholic Church*, after declaring the law
that Catholics who have committed mortal sin should not receive
Communion without having first received sacramental absolution,
follows that last statement with the word "unless" (no. 1457). This
makes it perfectly clear, first of all, that the Church believes sins can
be forgiven without Confession; otherwise there could be no "unless."
The *Catechism* goes on to say we are obligated to confess before
Communion unless two conditions are realized. The first is that we
have a "grave reason" for receiving Communion. Given the nature and
value of Communion as the Body and Blood of Jesus Christ, and the
fact that Jesus said, "Unless you eat the flesh of the Son of Man and
drink his blood, you have no life in you" (John 6:53), it would seem that
this condition always exists. The second condition is that there is "no
possibility" of going to Confession. In the mind of the Church, who is
always a loving mother, "no possibility" is not absolute. For example, if a
woman guilty of adultery is at Mass and longing for reconciliation and
Communion, and there is a priest right there sitting in the confessional,
no bishop in the Catholic Church would say it was "possible" for her to
go to Confession to him if he were her son! She should ask pardon from
God, receive Communion, and confess her sin when another priest
is available. The same argument would apply to other cases when, for
special reasons, a person might find it morally impossible to confess to a
particular priest who is available. The sad truth is that some confessors
might do us more harm than good.

APPENDIX

1. See, for example, John Henry Newman's distinction between "notional" and "real" knowledge in his *Grammar of Assent.*

2. From an interview quoted in the *National Catholic Reporter*, Sept. 4, 2009, p. 6.

3. Canon 915. Most Catholics — and many priests — do not know that, since the new Code of Canon Law abolished the excommunication that was formerly attached to marriages unrecognized by the Church, there is nothing in Canon Law that forbids those "married out of the Church" to receive Communion. This is not a "legal" matter, but a matter of conscience to be worked out with one's confessor.

4. Exhortation after the Synod on "Reconciliation and Penance in the Mission of the Church," paragraph 9.

5. Cyprian's Epistle 53 at http://www.newadvent.org/fathers/050653. htm.

OF RELATED INTEREST

Forgiveness
One Step at a Time
JOSEPH A. SICA

Here Father Joe Sica offers ten invaluable steps to help readers take forgiveness seriously, and he choreographs them to connect with Jesus' gospel teachings.

152 PP | $12.95 | ORDER 957620 | 978-1-58595-762-0

Finding Our Sacred Center
A Journey to Inner Peace
HENRI NOUWEN

Struggling to find peace of heart, Henri Nouwen visited Lourdes. Whether you have been there or not does not matter: This journal will touch your own restless and searching heart and help you find again your own sacred center. A wonderful and beautiful gift book!

HARDCOVER | 64 PP | $9.95 | ORDER 958474 | 978-1-58595-847-4

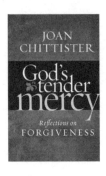

God's Tender Mercy
Reflections on Forgiveness
JOAN CHITTISTER

Sister Joan's insights invite readers to seek holiness through receiving and then offering God's tender mercy and forgiveness. In doing so they become holy. Reading this book is a wonderful spiritual journey to holiness through merciful forgiveness and genuine love of God and others.

HARDCOVER | 80 PP | $10.95 | ORDER 957996 | 978-1-58595-799-6

1-800-321-0411
www.23rdpublications.com